My Father Said
A Story About the
Accompong Maroons 1655-1738

Norma Rowe-Edwards

Emerge Publishing Group, LLC
Riviera Beach, FL
www.emergepublishers.com

Library of Congress Control Number:
20119299722

ISBN 978-976-95392-0-4

Front Cover design by
Lashonne Duncan Kellar

Published by
Emerge Publishing Group, LLC
Riviera Beach, Fl
www.emergepublishers.com

Norma Rowe-Edwards, 2011
My Father Said: A Story About the Accompong
Maroons 1655-1738 Norma Rowe-Edwards
1. History. 2. Reference

Printed in the United States of America

MY FATHER SAID

In memory of my father
who spent time to pass down oral history and
leave with us our positive identity as Africans called Maroons.
May you find a wealth of information within this book.

ACKNOWLEDGEMENTS:

There are so many individuals to thank. Without them this book would not have been possible. First, thanks to the Almighty God for the insight and strength to start this book.

Special thanks to my loving husband Alphonse who was a source of constant encouragement and to my grandsons who were always asking "Is the book ready?".

Thanks to:

Girzel Waite for giving me the title

Uncle Ivan who rekindled the passion of my father's beliefs

Ashley McFarlane, who worked diligently to make my thoughts come alive

Dr. Erna Brodber who asked the questions that helped me to bring clarity to the message.

Daynia Miles and Peter Anderson for enduring the many data entry revisions and corrections, hence the reality of this book. I consider myself blessed and highly favoured to have you all as a guide.

Also special thanks to the publisher, Emerge Publishing Group, LLC.

CONTENTS

INTRODUCTION

This book will tell the experiences of my African ancestors. It is not told from the perspective of world history as is written by Eurocentric scholars such as historians, lecturers, anthropologist or attorneys. The story I write is personal; it is not political. This writing is not an analysis of the life of my African ancestors. It is neither a comparison nor compilation of the ideas and stories of other historians. I will write what my father knew about our African ancestors. I will relate how my father used the events and all aspects of the battle between our ancestors and the British, to expose to us the character of my ancestors called Maroons. There is no doubt in my mind that my father's values echo those of many Africans then and now. What is important about Samuel's doctrine however was his determination to destroy the negative stereotyping of the Maroons. My hope is that the story of these experiences will focus the reader on the identity, character and aptitude of my African ancestors and add depth to what you may have read by others.

As I write I have one central difficulty; how to erase, and obliterate from my mind the inaccuracies others have written about us and continue to tell about us. If only my mind was a tabula rasa. If only I could rid my thoughts of the many discussions with learned scholars as they pull and compare the pieces of "history" written about us Maroons. If only I had the opportunity to write completely devoid of the mental contamination superimposed on my memory by the Maroon stories of others; then to write my father's story would be oh so easy. If only! Know that my attempt is to deliver as near and as is humanly possible an objective account of the atrocities experienced by my ancestors. However, more important is to extract from the stories the character of the people we now know as Maroons.

I am writing based on information given to me by my father, Samuel Nathaniel Rowe. I am an African descendant of the Trelawney Town Maroons Accompong State, in the island of Jamaica. I speak mainly of events surrounding my family; that is the children of Samuel Nathaniel Rowe and Irene Rowe, Nee Thomas. There is no doubt in my mind that similar experiences can be told by fellow Maroons in Accompong. Be aware that at that time there were three Maroon men from Trelawney Town, all carrying the name Samuel Rowe, two from Accompong and one from a nearby Maroon district in Thornton; however, only one was named Samuel Nathaniel Rowe; he was my father.

In this book, I will talk specifically about those African descendants who own the Cockpit Mountains in Jamaica and some of who now live in an area in the cockpit called Accompong. An Ashanti Medical Doctor recently advised me that "Achompong" is the correct spelling and not Accompong. Similarly, he also said that "Kojo" is the correct spelling of the Ashanti hero and not Cudjoe. Since this is not a research treatise, I will not spend time to research and validate this information. I will write from my Ashanti father's valuable account of his African ancestors who won the battle against the British. This battle lasted over eighty years. Nanny and Kojo were the master strategists. The battle ended after the British soldiers surrendered to my African ancestors. The British soldiers accepted the fact that my ancestors defeated them; a fact that highlights the strength of my ancestors.

The intent of this book is to release the identity of us Africans called Maroons, and to create a positive international perception with lasting legacy for our children. At the same time remove from our identity any debilitating image so designed by European, American and to some extent Caribbean scholars and writers. My hope is that this writing will help to clear the air and remove some of the misinformation that shrouds the identity of my ancestors and the Maroons of today.

As I write this story, I will use the events of the eighty-three years of resistance as the baseline from which I will extract the lessons that my father taught us. He was always telling us about the war and how our ancestors survived during those years. I sometimes grapple with the idea of whether to organize occurrences and the events of the time chronologically or to group them in by their importance and lessons of value. I find it also difficult to divorce the atrocity of the slave trade from the events of the struggle for freedom. How can I separate these? How is this possible when the aura of the atrocity lingers to this day? How can I capture the essence and spirit of the persons amidst the atrocity? An atrocity that burned deep into the core of the Ashanti, Coromante and Congo Africans in Jamaica West Indies and the Diaspora.

It was an atrocity that my ancestors used to purge the root of hate in them and instead awakened the spirit of self love. This love for self stirred their innate potential and made them victorious over their oppressors. The real significance of their history however, is lost in the records as others attempt to tell our story of a battle that engaged Africans defending themselves against the British militia; a battle that lasted for more than eighty years; a battle that the British lost. The battle remains shrouded by the entrapment of our identity as ascribed by others. Shrouded by a veil that covers the identity of a people, a veil called "Maroon." It is the story of "The Maroons." as told by others. I have read many stories written about the Maroons, some about my ancestors from Accompong. My willful omission of such stories helps me to keep my message clear as I present to you what my father knew about our ancestors the Maroons.

I will make some assumptions from my experiences with my father and my early years living in Accompong. The intent is to remove and destroy the veil that shrouds our identity as a people. The assumptions are not to trivialize the atrocities inflicted on my ancestors during the Atlantic Slave Trade and during their period of resistance. These assumptions will show how my ancestors survived the times and describe what made them successful. To you scholars, historians and researchers, I crave your indulgence, and understanding during this reading. My hope is that these assumptions will provoke your thoughts on the subject of the character and identity of the people called Maroons.

The text will speak of the period of resistance from 1655 to 1738-9. This book is not about "black", "brown" and "white." It is not about the people of African descent and the Europeans. Rather it is a book about the human race and the extent to which humankind will conjure up plots and tales to satisfy their insane ambition to dominate. It is a book that will remind us that the heart of man is desperately wicked or, should I say can be desperately wicked. It is a book that speaks to the power of hope. As you read this book, what will unfold to you is the covert plot to annihilate our Ashanti and Coromante and Congo ancestors, as well as their determination to survive and succeed

This book will not rehash the mayhem of the Atlantic Slave Trade but will extract from these dastardly acts a fresh portrait of who we are. It will disturb those who through no fault of their own, continue to document the language of others who label us as wild, pilferers, and guerillas. The book will help the reader to identify the character of the human commodity that was being traded, and in some instances being captured during The Atlantic Slave Trade; a commodity which some have come to know as Maroons.

Come sit with me as I share what was told to me by my father, a Maroon, who was born at the end of the 19th century and lived into the 20th century. Journey with me as some of my cousins, fellow Maroons, and I, peel away to reveal the identity of my ancestors. You will see the content of their character, their spirituality, courage, strength, determination, bravery, intelligence and wit. Be aware that Accompong Maroons are still guarded about our story. Many have come and have tasted of our hospitality and our culture. Many have written about us and yet there are still some things that we hold dear and that will remain untold to the "abinaqua". My father told me this is an African word for the non-Maroon. Pardon my spelling if it is incorrect. Remember, this is not a research document.

I still meet people who share with me what they believe to be a true picture of my ancestors and us Maroons. My father's aim was to indoctrinate us with the essential belief that we are spirit beings, capable of great feats. He saw to it that we understood the enormous power we have when we are truly connected to the Spirit of God and stand together united with God's Spirit. Daddy always reminded us that our world of endless possibilities comes when we are prepared and when our spirit is plugged into the Spirit of God. He imparted to us that we are not a people of deficiencies, but we are a people of innate differences. His desire was for his daughters to pass this knowledge to our children and hold them accountable for its onward transfer to all generations.

So why write now? Simple! The saying goes, "Nothing ever happens before the time." However, I write now because in the 21st Century, four centuries since my African ancestors the Maroons won the war against the British, we their descendants still remain silent about our powerful identity and history. I write because there are Jamaicans today who are unaware that the Maroons were free one hundred years before other Africans were emancipated in Jamaica. I write to refute all the nonsense about us. Maroons are not wild, untamed ugly people with red eyes, pudgy noses, and tails. In short, Maroons are not an exotic curiosity. That is not us. Yes, we have a TALE. It is a story of our heritage. It is not a romance novel. Samuel knew that and was determined that we likewise should know who we are. An old African proverb says, "Until the lion begins to write his own history, the tale of the hunt will always glorify the hunter." We must write our own history if not, others will write it for us.

In writing this book, it is not my intention to stimulate any debate, philosophical, ideological or otherwise. My hope is that the reader will travel with me through this journey in time. As I write from my experience among my family, I hope the reader will connect with the story of my people, the Ashanti Africans from Ghana, the Maroons.

1

WHO ARE THESE MAROONS?

For the first time, a true Maroon descendant of the Trelawney Town Maroons, Accompong State, will write the story of our African ancestors as passed down orally by her father. Other Maroons have written about the Maroon Story; however, this is the first story written by a Trelawney Town Maroon.

The Negro Slave Trade to the Caribbean started in 1503. Please take note that during that period the word "Maroon" used to describe my African ancestors as well as present day descendants is a word introduced by the Spanish slave owners from Hispaniola. The Africans were called "cimarrones" by the Spaniards because they would habitually flee to the mountains to escape being enslaved. This was the practice in Hispaniola. Later the British Colonels called the Africans Maroons.

Many scholars have deliberated as to the origin and meaning of the word Maroon. Whatever the source of the word, the meaning was not complimentary in my father's estimation and to him it was the epitome of cultural debasement. When I meet Jamaicans who are non-researchers, these Jamaicans have little knowledge of the people called Maroons. As I write and use the word "Maroon" throughout this book, please understand that my use of this word does not signify my endorsement of its use negative or otherwise. Moreover, as I use the word Maroon know that I am merely connecting the reader to the historical use of the word.

I present to you a people called Maroons, but let me hasten to make one thing very clear. My African ancestors, who were captured and taken to Jamaica and other parts of the world during the Atlantic Slave Trade, were not wild savages; they were civilized people. In Jamaica, Maroon was the name given to those of my ancestors who were enslaved by the Spanish, and who did not run away with them to Cuba when the English captured Jamaica from the Spaniards in 1655. These ancestors instead settled in the mountains in the East and West of the Island from where they successfully waged guerilla warfare against the English settlers and British Militia. The British surrendered in 1738.

The name Maroon was not the only label conferred on my African ancestors. They were also described as Ashanti warriors presumably because of their tribal origins in Africa. While they were in Africa, they were never known as Maroons. When I think of maroon, I connect the word with "marooned" as in isolated. For instance, if you are shipwrecked and suddenly find yourself on one of the Cays, at a place where you are alone, isolated, and no one knows that you are there or in sight to rescue you, then you are indeed marooned. This physical positioning makes you a maroon. In the eyes of their captors, the Africans "ran away to the mountains and because they were "cut off from civilization", they were marooned. Likewise, escape from mountains was not an option for my ancestors they were therefore marooned.

The name Maroon that persists today, however, is used to describe descendants of Africans who were not killed by the Spanish, and who were successful in their defense against the assault and attack of the British militia. The existence of the many Maroon communities throughout the island speaks to their successful resistance against enslavement. I believe these Maroon communities throughout the western and eastern parts of Jamaica, speak to what must have been the concurrent movement of resistance that was widespread throughout enslaved communities in the Caribbean and the Diaspora.

I speak as a Leeward Maroon, of Trelawney Town, Accompong State, Jamaica West Indies. Know that there are other Jamaican Maroons in Flagstaff, Flamstead, Scotts Hall, Moore Town, Charles Town and Clarke's Town and many other places, especially throughout the entire Cockpit Country. To my fellow Maroons in those communities not mentioned, note that your exclusion from this writing is only circumstantial. It bears no significance to our struggle, the African struggle. Recently a group of Maroons in Flagstaff has identified Flagstaff as the place where the Peace Treaty was signed. This information is incorrect and only serves to confuse the ignorant. My father and I can only speak of the Accompong Town Maroons. I will talk about the other Maroons in the other Maroon communities and their connection to the Accompong Maroons as their involvement relates to the struggle against the British settlers.

Samuel was born one hundred and sixty years, four generations after the battle ended and the Peace Treaty was signed at Accompong in 1738. This Treaty between the Leeward Maroons and the British was signed on March 1, 1738. He lived his life as a continuing expression and account of his ancestors. His life was an open storybook, with highlights and marks that underlined and portrayed graphic descriptions of his people. It contained descriptions of a strong, brave people, with wit, honesty, good character and above all a people plugged in and connected to the spirit of God. They were a people of African descent called Maroons by those who brutalized them. Samuel's every word, every glance, every pause, every smile every stare, every frown, every pensive mood, was delivered as if he was an eyewitness to the life, struggle and battle of our ancestors as they mounted their defense against the British oppressors, the British militia and the British settlers.

You need not question his portrayal of our ancestors' life story. He was the storyteller and his desire was to articulate the essence of the story with accuracy. It was not a story of panic or fear or self-pity. It was a story of a proud people with fortitude. He never shared the stage with anyone as he told the story. You may call him selfish; however I believe he wanted to be sure that the message of this important story was not lost in the script of any writer.

Samuel wanted to drive home to us how important and powerful we Maroons are. He wanted to leave with us a strong, solid account of the Maroon struggle and use these experiences to mold an indelible inscription in our minds, an inscription that would become the fundamental building blocks in the development of our thoughts our character and our spirit. The character and life of my father will form the backdrop for my discussion throughout this book. I will use his personality, lifestyle, beliefs and stories to connect you with our ancestors: to connect you with who we are.

The stories in this writing are as my father related them to my sisters and me. The life lessons given to my father by his elders, and transferred from him to us, were the lessons of a very resourceful people who were full of energy and a determination to succeed. The legacy and value of these lessons to us from my African ancestors and my father transcends the mere telling of historical Maroon stories; stories, to me that often seem to distract us from the character and fortitude of my ancestors and forget about the knowledge of their spiritual connection. He told us what he knew about our ancestors and what he knew about the war. His stories of them framed the masterpiece as he painted the picture of a people at war, and a people rising to success. He painted a picture of a people who were hardworking. It is through his story of the war that I will find resonance with my ancestors as I see them. My father was adept in the delivery of his reports to us. The focus in his stories to us was the success of our African ancestors in the struggle against the British. He wanted to leave us with a clear positive image of our ancestors. I believe that it is for this reason that he made a choice not to focus on the middle passage; that is the passage from Africa to Jamaica.

For too long others have misrepresented us, guessed our ancestry, and have attempted to disprove our sovereignty. We, the descendants of our Ashanti African ancestors, who won the struggle against the British, are a Sovereign people. The Trelawney Town Maroons Accompong State is a sovereign State on the Island of Jamaica. My ancestors were not all runaway slaves. Most were people freed by the Spanish and who choose to live in `the mountainous areas of Portland, Clarendon, and the Cockpit Country. It is therefore reasonable to take the position that the present descendants living in Accompong and the Diaspora are not runaways neither were our ancestors.

I find that it is difficult for me to enter into my imaginary world of captivity. The one thing that I can relate to is the sight of a frantic caged bird. I reflect on the sight of the captured bird roving to and fro in its new domesticated home, a cage, and pacing frantically looking for that route of escape to freedom. It is then that I wonder what first went through the minds of my ancestors. I want to believe that they wanted to be free. I believe that the pursuit of freedom must have been paramount on their minds during their passage from Africa to Jamaica.

I recognize that while they were in transit, the execution of a movement of resistance was not an option for them. Where would they escape to, in the ocean? The historians report that some Africans jumped overboard while in transit to their destinations away from Africa. Once they arrived on land however, I am sure their choice was to keep the only two things that were in their control, their minds and their spirits free.

I cannot imagine what went through their minds. I believe that while they were huddled and chained together in the belly of the ships, they nurtured and developed the spirit of unity and the drive to overcome this ordeal. I believe that amidst the stench of their environment in the slave ships, they were able to adopt and embrace the positive power of the Spirit that was inherent in each of them. It was not an evil spirit. It was the Spirit of God. It was their understanding of the omnipotent power of the Spirit of God that strengthened their human capacity to succeed without compromise.

I believe their motto must have been all for one and one for all. I believe they could not allow any greed, arrogance, selfishness or bitterness to enter their spirit. I believe that each knew his potential and recognized the energy of unity.

I wonder how they coped as they lay chained together deprived of their freedom. The freedom to move around; to see other than what was overhead or a mere glance to their left, and right. What was the visual like? Were there even any familiar sounds? How then did they cope? I believe that their environment forced them to develop coping skills instantly. Skills that I deduce were ingrained and developed during their passage from Africa.

Some will find this imposed adventure difficult to understand and I sympathize with them. To those people, I believe it is the insanity of their ignorance that drives them to make irresponsible conclusions about the history of my African ancestors. They want to reduce our ancestors, their experience and their victory against the British to something not commendable; to reduce them to being runaways and traitors. Some of these writers want to depict my ancestors as wild, and ferocious. Moreover there is a subtle transfer of these traits to present day Maroons.

The capture and enslavement of my ancestors was an atrocity. There was no doubt about that, for these Africans to win the battle against the British militia they had to be brilliant, shrewd and disciplined. It was an astronomical feat. My father wanted us to not only grasp the reality of the events but also experience the pulse of our African ancestors as they fought for freedom; the freedom of which I am a beneficiary.

When my father shared the story of the Atlantic crossing of our ancestors, he had little to say except, "they captured them like dogs, beat them, chained them and sent them off." I believe that his deliberate brevity and omission on the subject was his way to direct our thoughts to the character and mission of our ancestors. Hence, his responsibility to us was to hammer in and drive home to us the depth of spirit and true significance of our ancestors from Africa. He wanted us to know that the same Spirit that was resident in our ancestors was also resident in us.

On all accounts by Samuel, these Africans were strangers in their homeland. The one thing common among them was captivity. How then did they come together? It is for this reason that I believe my African ancestors must have developed survival skills. What came first? I believe that a system of communication was the first skill developed by them. A code of communication must have been an essential requirement for survival. We know that man's inability to communicate effectively is directly related to his ability to succeed.

Consider that you have just spent months in the belly of a ship. Your future is unknown. The time to disembark on new territory is now. You will have new rules to obey. You will live wherever your master determines. The gift to choose is not yours; however, the door of the cage is open. There is no doubt in my mind that their choice of living in the mountainous and densely forested areas of the island was not accidental. The mountain range of Jamaica is visible from all shores. I believe that on disembarking, geographic location was a requisite to their strategic plan of freedom. On landing they must have been thinking, maybe we will get to those mountains some way somehow. Those mountains will provide a way of escape at the right time. It would be foolish to believe that any movement of resistance would be successfully implemented while in the plains of Jamaica. How then were all these ideas discussed? Who developed the code and language of communication?

As I mentioned earlier, Accompong is the birthplace of my father, Samuel, and the final battlefield between our African ancestors and the British militia. It is the place where Nanny and Kojo were declared winners of the war against the British. Samuel said Accompong was formerly called Trelawney Town, Maroon Town, then Nanny Town, later Accompong Nanny Town and now Accompong. The Cockpit Mountains of North Western Jamaica and the mountains of Portland were the prime venue for combat between the British soldiers and my ancestors. It was there in the Cockpit Mountains in Accompong, Jamaica that Kojo the African Commander in Chief signed the Leeward Treaty in March 1, 1738. Some months later, the Windward Treaty was signed in 1739.

From the early age of four years, my sister Una and I were

introduced to the African experience in Accompong. I was the second of four children, all of whom were girls. My older sister Una was two years my senior. Patricia and Millicent came later. My father would share his stories with each of us. Because I was the second eldest, I had the privilege of hearing about my ancestors repeatedly. This is an experience that is indelible in my mind; one that is never to be erased or trivialized; the significance of my African ancestors living in Accompong, Jamaica. It was here in Accompong that I connected with the spirit of my African ancestors called Maroons.

Many Jamaicans have asked me the question "Why am I a Jamaican and yet not identified as a Maroon"? Moreover, "what makes you a Maroon"? As far as Samuel was concerned, a Maroon was a biological descendant of the Ashanti Africans and other Africans who fought in the battle against British. What does it mean to be a Maroon? From my father's standpoint, being a Maroon means being an individual of a special breed distinct from any other breed, culture or class of people in the world. My father painted a picture of my African Maroon ancestors as a people who would fight at all cost to retain what they believe was theirs. In the case of my ancestors, it was their right to freedom, their dignity and their self respect. They were not beggars. They were hardworking people who believed in their right to freedom. My ancestors demonstrated this right to freedom long before the American Constitution proclaimed; "We hold these truths to be self evident….." It was a right deprived of them when they were forcefully removed from the land of their birth. When they became the means to satisfy the greed, indifference and injustice of an economic system called capitalism.

As you read my story, I sincerely hope that your questions will be answered as to what makes one a Maroon. Through my life's journey thus far, I have been blessed with the opportunity to experience a glimpse of other transplanted Africans in different parts of the Diaspora. I have met some of my fellow Maroon Africans from Suriname. I hope that the reader will capture the identity of our people through what is written in this book. It was an identity so ably described by Thomas Clarkson.

These people from the Ashanti, Coromante and Congo tribes, though brought here involuntary, came with a duty to self and a commitment to love. They must have played a mental tape that kept repeating, 'My duty is to return to my free self." It was a duty that, I believe, became an obsession. They came with their spirit, history, their pride, and education. They had a full command of their native language and later developed a language for success, "patois", which was a mix, I believe, of Spanish, English, Ashanti and Coromante. They came with skills. They were builders, and they used their skills to build their mud huts and wattle and daub houses. They were masons, bricklayers, blacksmiths, carpenters, engineers, barbers, tailors, dressmakers and chefs, to name a few. They were teachers, nurses, doctors, pharmacists, judges, and lawyers of their time, albeit without an alma mater. Theirs was a "non traditional" school of education where graduates stayed connected in their informal way. They were crafts men and women who crossed the Atlantic without their tools yet they manufactured products.

They were hunters and some were soldiers, not wild ferocious warriors. If they were not transported from Africa with these skills, then it must be that at some time during their time here they learned everything that was necessary for them to adapt and succeed. It must have been difficult for them to be hunted by the British soldiers. They were not stupid. They came with a very developed religious system. I believe that the King James Version of the Bible did not influence their knowledge of their African identity. This knowledge of who they were, was cemented in their determination to recapture their freedom at all cost. These assumptions will be borne out as I write about the struggle for freedom.

Nanny and Kojo represent the qualities and character of Ashanti Africans. They demonstrated the reward of participation, the benefits of preparation, the application of faith and the wisdom to plan. They understood the true meaning of "United we stand divided we fall." My father described to me a Kojo and a Nanny who were brave, strong and intelligent leaders. They had the responsibility to deliver a people into freedom and with the help of the almighty God, they did.

My father was a great, great, great grandson of the Ashanti freedom fighters. He was determined to leave us with the legacy of who we are and the drive to fight to continue to be who we are as Maroons. I hope other Maroons will share with the world our legacy as we lift the beliefs and altruism of our ancestors.

Accompong, the Capital of the Leeward Maroon community, boasts a legacy that must be articulated to all. This legacy, that is more than the land bequeathed to us, is a legacy of a strong free spirit.

2

HIS MOMENT, MY MOMENT, OUR MOMENT

There is so much to tell about my Maroon ancestors and especially my life with my father Bah (brother) Sam an indomitable Maroon man. Samuel was no ordinary Maroon, no ordinary man; he was special. My father was a descendant of Africans who successfully resisted captivity by the British militia. They were the first Freedom fighters in the Western Hemisphere. They won an eighty-three year battle against the British. Land was formally ceded to these Africans as part of their Treaty settlement in 1738-39 and Accompong Town officially became the seat of government of the Maroons. Accompong is to Trelawny Town Maroons as Gordon House is to Jamaica. What then was so special about this Maroon named Samuel Nathaniel Rowe from Accompong? It was his determination to pass on to us the depth of character and the significance of our African ancestors, the Freedom Fighters who won their battle against the British imperial army.

Samuel told me he was a descendant of the Ashanti tribe from the Gold Coast of West Africa, now called Ghana and his Ashanti ancestors were captured in Africa and taken to Jamaica to be slaves on the plantations. Such was the fate of millions of Africans during the Trans Atlantic Slave Trade, some of whom were sold into slavery and deposited to other parts of the Caribbean and North and South America. The slave owners' purpose was to use them to provide free labour whether they were in the Caribbean or the American mainland. Samuel said that in Jamaica the Africans were slaves who worked on the plantation. Therefore, it makes sense to assume that during those times, wherever you found a plantation in Jamaica you would also find African slaves.

According to Ashanti custom, a leader was being groomed at all times. The passing of the baton was an Ashanti custom. The patriarch appointed the oldest male child to be coached in the position of leader. It seems as if in this Ashanti tradition, this passing of the baton, was designated to the first-born male. Samuel, first-born male in his family, was therefore coached and tutored by his father James Rowe. It was now time for him to pass on this responsibility of keeping the trust and providing leadership to his children.

As far as my father was concerned and in keeping with the tradition, there should always be a leader being prepared be it a male or a female. My older sister Una was therefore the apparent heir of this position in my family. The expectations and directions from Samuel were simple. He expected her to show her ability to take on the duty of caring for the younger siblings in the event of his demise.

When Samuel could not find the tie from her spirit to continue this tradition, he turned to me to take on the leadership role. What was this show of caring ability that Samuel expected? I am not sure to this day that I know and neither will I guess. What my sisters and I noticed was that he later began to call on me more often. We noticed this subtle gradual shift as the leadership moved from my older sister to me. He called me to find out if we had completed our homework; he called to check our plans for extra curricula activities. It was my responsibility to tell him when the Youth Catholic Organization (CYO) would meet at the Rectory. Samuel wanted to continue this tradition. He was graceful and informal with the process as he turned to me to take on the leadership role. It was now my job to be the "leader-in-training". My father did not ask questions. I did not apply for this responsibility. I was just next in line. I believe that he would have directed his choice to my younger sister if I did not assume my responsibilities or meet his requirements.

Samuel did not sit us down to lecture. He did not have a curriculum. He knew from our ancestors that we must take care of our own. It was therefore his responsibility to apply this philosophy to his daughters and hope for us to pass on the information to our children.

As I ponder the idea of writing about father's Ashanti influence in my life, I keep remembering the day in the summer in 1949. This was a special day for my father. It was the day that my father would witness his little seven-year-old acting on stage at the prestigious Ward Theatre. This day should also be special for me. But, oh! What a dilemma was I in! I was in a stew then and did not quite know how to get out.

At the tender age of seven who would expect me to get out of any stew anyhow? By the standards of behavior set in those days, I doubted my ability to voice my predicament or settle my quandary. "Children must have respect and discipline" was my father's favourite saying. "Respect and discipline will take you a far way." Respect or no respect, discipline or no discipline, I was perplexed.

Through the corner of one eye I glanced at my father in the rocking chair, not rocking, just patiently waiting for my mother to complete the last minute detail of combing my "picky picky dry head" (colloquial for short hair). I was afraid to look at him. If I did, I would see his expression and be forced to respond to him. My father had soft curly wooly black hair. My hair was short and had length enough to afford my mother the freedom and luxury to part and twist only a small section of hair at a time. Over the years of combing my hair and after the many sessions at this task, my mother developed the skill of twisting and combing my hair. I, therefore, did not mind her repeated maneuvers to make the twist hold. Her repetitive actions of rolling the hair between thumb and forefinger helped my desire to delay my readiness.

My mother was doing her best on this day to groom me for my acting debut. She was oblivious of the fact that her seemingly delay was to my benefit. In addition, my father was as proud as a peacock as he waited for her to add the final touch.

My father was patiently waiting for me. My mother had my head cocked at the neck with just enough of an angle to help her accomplish her task. At a quick half glance, not lifting my head but merely moving my eyeballs to look in his direction, I noticed he was not smiling. I hardly remember my father engaged in any laughter. Oh yes! One time, when his first grandchild Kay went outside the house and bought ice cream from an itinerant ice cream vendor. Kay was three years at the time. It was 1965. She was born on the day of Jamaica's Independence.

That evening when my mother and sister arrived home my father reported the story thus: *"me poah bwoy was sitting inside reading the bible and she come inside and give me the ice cream and said, take this. She was eating ice cream tuh. Me never even si wen shi come out a di house or hear the ice cream man ring him bell. Me soh friten all a could duh is ask her whey she get the money from to buy the ice cream. Shi jus tell mi, eat it and don't ask any question. Mi poah bwoy jus have to eat it."*

My sister Millie reported that Samuel was hysterical when he reported the incident. He laughed until his false teeth almost fell out of his mouth. As I recall my father always spoke the Queens' prim and proper English and if I am not mistaken, I heard of him speaking patois this first and last time. He must have been frightened out of his drawers trying to understand how a grandchild of his could leave his presence without his knowing. Or, was he hysterical because his first grandchild was demonstrating true Maroon independent qualities? Hmm!

He sat in the rocking chair just waiting for me. He wore on his face an inimitable expression. It was seemingly stern yet compassionate, direct yet personable, compelling yet tactful, questioning yet loving, sharp yet caring. Without asking him a question, you read his facial expression and with accuracy could foretell the meaning of the non-verbal message he was trying to convey at that moment. He was a genius in facial choreography. His characters came alive at the bat of an eyelid. When he talked about our ancestors dressing themselves in cocoon leaves and hiding among foliage his eyes were half closed and his shoulder curved. After careful scrutiny of his face, I learned how to interpret the meaning of some of these expressions. He sat patiently waiting for my mother to complete her task of getting me dressed and prepared to leave for the Ward Theatre.

Samuel was born in August 1898, one hundred and sixty years after his African ancestors signed the Peace Treaty with the British Government. Even at the age of seven, I remember the expression on my father's face as he waited for my mother to complete the task of combing my hair. His expression reminded me of the many stories he told me about those stern African ancestors of ours. They were Africans labeled Maroons, a name given to them by the English colonists who terrorized them in the Cockpit Mountains and other areas of Jamaica. Theirs was a fight for some eighty-three years, a fight to stay free. This evening in July, I saw in my father's expression the likes of an austere Kojo. I fear the man.

Kojo was the African Commander-in-Chief who my father described to me so many times. It is amazing that at the age of seven I somehow was able to connect my father's many stories about Kojo and Nanny and see them as real before me. I began to think of the character of this firm ruler Kojo and started to ask myself the question; Is it possible for me to witness the trait of Kojo come to life in my father's demeanor? I was told the stories of the war and heard many times about Kojo, Nanny, and Nina that the existence of these ancestors became a living part of me. When I reflect on the stories and saw my father's facial expression, I became petrified. What if I am right? Kojo and Nanny, as reported to me by my father, were no-nonsense people. They were smart, determined, resourceful and disciplined.

I have never seen my father like this, just there in the chair almost motionless. For a fleeting moment, I managed to take a quick but good look at him to read his mood. This time I turned my head in his direction and looked at him. I did not quite know what I would do with the information or how my little mind would process it. I was only concerned about his seemingly non-verbal and perhaps non-threatening posture.

We were not allowed to stare at an adult. Samuel said to stare at an adult was bad manners. I doubt that any information at that time would help me to make any useful decision that would guide my next action. Any action I feared on my part would evoke the wrath of my father, if ever that were possible. I have never seen my father angry. He talked about determination but never connected anger as a perquisite for realizing ones goal.

My father was ready to go. My mother had completed her artistry in my hair and had finished the final touches and secured the bow at the back of my costume.

The costume was a long and bright floral orange frock with a round neck and puffed sleeves. In today's' style language, you probably would describe the sleeves as bouffant. The skirt was gathered at the waistline and had streamers that would finish as a big bow in the back. The frock flowed all the way down to the floor. To this day this costume and the events of that evening are as vivid as ever in my mind. What took place that evening cemented in my mind an indelible picture of what must have been a Maroon's pride, courage and firmness. The time had come. I must now move away from my mother's artistry and get out of the house to the Ward Theatre. I must play my part in the School Play, "Tom-Tit-Tot". My father was ready to leave.

My mother was finished preparing me for the event. Nothing more was left for her to do. The hour was now at hand. Only I did not know if I would glorify my father or if I would suffer his wrath and be sent on to glory. I really could not tell then if he would be patient nor could I tell if he would be angry with me. I knew I was afraid of that moment.

Maroons were known to be no nonsense people. My father told me on many occasions how serious, skillful and determined Kojo, Nanny and my other ancestors were. Samuel told us that Kojo would cut off the heads of those who were not loyal to the cause of securing freedom for all. Kojo had zero tolerance for traitors or non-performers.

Although I had practiced my part in the play and felt I was prepared, I was definitely not ready that day for the event. Would I ever be ready? I hardly thought so. Not if I have to wear this costume on the street. I did not have a clue that I would be expected to wear a long dress as my costume. Most of all I must wear it on the street? I was well versed with the few words I had to say. This costume was the problem. I would have to walk from home, on Beeston Street, to the Ward Theatre. There was no other way for us to get to the Ward Theatre. No bus traveled from Beeston Street to Parade. My father didn't drive nor owned a car. He would not ask his only relative with a car. No sir! He was too independent and wanted to teach us how not to depend on others; unless of course there was a mission to accomplish and interdependence was the road to success. Settle with what you have. "Use what you have."

This was essentially one of the golden rules of our African ancestors. Don't envy people for what they have because if you know how they got it you might not want it. Samuel was a teacher and taught us well. He did not have a friend with a car. How then would we get to the Ward Theatre? He had already invited the whole world as far as I was concerned. I was in a predicament. Surely now something here really needed some sorting out. This little seven-year-old girl, "country bumpkin, country come to town", must wear this long dress on the street. After all, why should I dress as some old country woman to perform an insignificant part in this play? In those days girls my age wore skirts that were a little below the knees.

As I recall, the story of Tom-Tit-Tot was not a children's play. It was a play about adults where children were acting out adult roles. It seems that my father's concern was this exposure and soon to be, acme of my short-lived acting career. If my predicament did not change, the star would not be born. I was embarrassed. My long dress was the centre of my embarrassment. The style was not for my age at that time. No child my age would be seen on the street in such attire. If I could have found a way to disappear and let the whole episode pass, then I would have. I was saturated in embarrassment. At the time, Nanny's spiritual powers were foreign to me. Samuel was careful in his discussions about our ancestors. He shared with us only what we were able to grasp independent of any explanation.

I had recently returned from Accompong Maroon Town where the older women wore long dresses most of the time. On Sundays, they would dress up as I was on this summer day. The only addition for some of these women's Sunday attire was a big white head wrap that spiraled on their heads, ending with a bump in the front of the head and one or two pencils from under the wrap. The pencils were at the temple and visible above the ear. I was told that the revival missionary believes that an individual messenger is assigned to each revivalist and therefore the revivalist dresses accordingly. The pencils are for note taking as the message comes forth while the person is in the spirit. I surely did not see the revivalist with a notepad. My Aunts Betsy and Sister Mac did not dress with the pencils stuck in under their head wrap. Sister Mac was my aunt. I cannot say why we did not call her Aunt. I only know that my father, and his brother, Uncle Israel. Aunt V, Uncle Levi and Uncle Selvin all called her "Coolie Gal". We dared not call her by that name to her face. Respect and discipline would not allow us to forget her title. All sorts of images started to pass through my mind as I pondered what to do next.

The first thought that came to my mind was our first trip to Accompong. It was my first trip on the Jamaica Railway Train from Kingston to Maggotty. My father and mother traveled with my sister and me to the Railway Station in Kingston. Sister Mac and my cousin Vernal were the designated chaperones to travel with us to Accompong. They lived in Accompong and had just ended a visit with us in Kingston. I was not anxious that I was leaving my father and mother. Uncle Vernal, as I called him and Sister Mac were not strangers to us. Our parents came on board the train with us and in no time Samuel was engaged in a conversation with some stranger he had just met. He had no difficulty engaging in dialogue. Although it was difficult for me to hear, I am almost sure he was sharing his Maroon story and heritage. That legacy was his lifeline.

While he chatted, Sister Mac sat muttering to herself all the time. I thought something was the matter with her, except the expression on her face was as if someone was listening intently to her. Every now and then, her entire body gave a sudden jolt forward and backwards as if an electrical current charged through her body. At the same time, the mutterings ended in a low moan and a slight jerk of the body with a shake of her head. My sister and I had seen this motion at home. We settled ourselves besides her anxiously awaiting our first train ride to Accompong. Samuel was confident that the Ashanti family ties and commitment to unity was strong enough to sustain us during this period of separation. Who has a better understanding of separation than descendants of the Maroons? I knew that my father's level of comfort and trust in his sisters and nephew was unquestionable.

Soon there was a loud noise and the train conductor shouted something. I heard metal clonking and saw smoke ahead. The smoke had a peculiar odour that filled the metal cars of the train. Samuel and my mother had already left the train and were ready to walk home. My sister and I sat closer together as they departed to the platform. I sat at the window seat and looked as the train slowly pulled away from the station. I was comforted immediately as I realized that my Uncle Vernal was sitting next to me. Sister Mac was in another seat with my sister Una sitting beside her.

I remember the train going through what seemed to be a long dark tunnel. I listened to its wheels as they made a loud rhythmic grinding sound; it was a sound that matched the side-to-side rock of the train. I loved every bit of this. Each clackity-clack of the train wheels moved us closer to our destination; closer to "The Country". The destination will be Accompong, a quiet country where we were sheltered and nurtured by the togetherness and spirit of family.

I longed to be with my cousins. I wanted to play with them at the river. I wanted to play the ring games, hide-and-seek. The many trees in Aunt Betsy's yard gave me more than enough hiding places. The only obstacle was that my cousins knew all the possible places that we could hide. They had the advantage. Ashanti principle however dictated to me that my mission was to find the way to win the battle. Not even the creeping, crawling sometimes-jumping creatures were in my radar. I cherished playtime especially when the ground was wet and slippery after the rain.

There was something about the smell of fresh wet clay. The aroma made me feel as if it was something to eat. I yearned for the opportunity to play house with our corn stick dolls. Yes, we made dolls from dried corncob. Our little angels, corn stick dolls, were decked in clothes made from the corn trash and natural silky hair cascade from the top of the corn. These little creatures were handmade by us; that is "made in Jamaica" by my sister and my cousins. We used every part of the corn except the stalk to complete our own personal little person. We were wrapped in the personality of our dolls as we played and tried to mimic our older relatives. Most times, we played revival church. I liked to play church because there was a feeling of supremacy as we beat the drum and spun around each other.

Aunt Betsy and Sister Macs' pastime was praying and talking to God. They were always praying and getting in the spirit even when washing clothes at the river. It seems they were always connected to the Spirit of God. I called my doll Nen Nen. Nen Nen was the name of one of my aunts who was deceased. I cannot say why I chose that name. Aunt Betsy talked about her with such love and affection; maybe that's why I gave my doll that name. We were allowed to play only with my other cousins who lived near Grave wood. Others we met at school or at church. That is why we loved the street meetings because this event gave us an opportunity to be outdoors and at the same time to learn about spiritual worship.

Home in Accompong was a two-room wooden mansion. It was the family nest of the matriarch, Elizabeth Salmon, formerly Elizabeth Rowe, affectionately known to all as Aunt Betsy. The house had two rooms. One room was for dining and the other was for sleeping. The wallpaper, a collage of pages from old magazines and newspapers, covered the walls of the rooms from the floor to the ceiling. Even the windows were covered with the wallpaper. My auntie applied the wallpaper with such artistry that it made the rooms feel alive and warm.

Strong wood provided flooring. The floor was manicured daily with a mixture of red ox dye. I remember my cousin sweeping the floor, washing it with cloth and water, then rubbing on the dye and spreading it evenly on the wooden floor. All this was such fun to us. We watched her as she meticulously rubbed each grain of wood with the polish. Next came the fun part, the preparation of the coconut brush, "the buffing machine". I loved that part! Why was this so? I believe only because it required the use of fire. My cousin would take a piece of live firewood and guide it over the face of the coconut brush. This heat melts the wax and makes the preparation ready for application to the floor. As she polishes the wood with the coconut brush, she had a particular rhythm and a song. She was down on her knees with her behind in the air. With each push of the coconut brush, she combined the rub of the brush with a thud on the floor, a song, and a rhythm as if she was playing a drum. All this she did to add sheen and beauty to the finished detail of the floor. The floor was so shiny you could "see your face in it." This popular Jamaican expression was used to describe, "clean".

Two wooden steps and a wooden door provided access to the house. A wooden window was in each room and when Auntie closed the windows, the rooms were in total darkness. Except for the moonlight that seeped through the rare crack from an occasional imperfect joint in the wood; the place was dark. Aunt Betsy made sure that every crack was covered with old newspaper. She attacked every crack with her homemade paste and wallpaper. Nightfall was not a welcome time indoors. The rooms were dark. It was so dark that inside the room felt heavy. Aunt Betsy's house was demolished however; a similar house still stands in the Accompong community. That house is the home of my Uncle Vernal.

The kitchen was outdoors and behind the house. This important family room made from stone with a zinc roof and dirt floor boasts a built-in firewall from where the most nutritious, exquisite traditional meals were cooked and served. Fire was made from firewood. This part of the house was off limits to my sister and me. Aunt Betsy always had salted pork and cow tripe hanging over the fireplace. She placed a pan under the meat to catch the drippings of oil from the pork. Because the kitchen was so near to the house, the smell of smoke hung on everything inside and outside. The pillow, the sheets, the clothing even the floor mat. Even the water boiled on the wood fire had a taste of smoke. I call it barbecue water. Kush Kush twig was used between the clothing but that did little to offset the smell of the smoke. I love that smell.

The toilet was a distance away from the house. Its location from the house and the natural privacy from the trees and shrubs made it a creepy place. Inside was always dark and I cringed every time I had to go there. My cousins seemed comfortable with their experience in there. My level of comfort would only come after the motion was completed. There were several cracks in the wooden wall. I knew them all. Each became my locus while in the "little house". I forced my cousin to remain outside the toilet until I was finished. Gross! Maybe to the reader it seems that way. Remember that in Ashanti custom the older protects the younger. The house, the kitchen and the toilet formed the nucleus of what we called home. The warmth and love of family was beyond the wooden structures and the stone kitchen. The spirit was alive between our neighbours and us. We surely lived as one family.

Aunt Betsy's house was typical of the architecture in Accompong at that time. I remember there were two big houses in Accompong, two shops, a bakery and one building that housed the church and school. We walked to school, to church to the river and everywhere we went. We did not stay outdoors late after dark because it was dark. I was afraid of "Town Master". Town Master was the name given to Kojo and his spirit was known to travel on a donkey along the road at nights. We were all afraid of Town Master.

I never figured out how Aunt Betsy and Uncle Vernal survived. I do know that they had all kinds of fruit trees, sugar cane, yam, coco, dasheen, breadfruit, and ackee. Uncle Vernal would take the ground provisions to the market at Maggotty. My sister and I went with Uncle Vernal in our private limo, a donkey called tazer. We sat one in each hamper. What a ride. When Uncle Vernal came to Town, my father would supply flour and other goods for him to take to the country. The folks in the Country used to sing this: "When brother Vernal come from Town we will have flour, flour to serve us till we dead." It was a simple song that described the spirit of community and sharing.

Now as I reminisce, I realize that my ancestors were not as fortunate as I. Imagine being removed from home, Africa, forcefully and taken on a blind journey to an unknown destination. Add to that your fate as a slave and then try to fathom your plight. It seems difficult. Suddenly I was jolted back to reality when I realized that my mother was no longer combing my hair. The memory faded.

My father was ready to go. I knew by the look on his face. He did not seem to understand that his little girl although fully dressed, was not ready. I was not mentally up to this assignment. I started to think about my performance of the previous night. Oh! Was I shocked when my teacher gave my father the dress at the end of the rehearsal and told him that I had to wear the costume to the theatre. That was the first time I was exposed to this long dress and the fact that I was expected to wear it on the street. It did not matter that I earned some sophisticated chuckles as I performed and said my few words at the dress rehearsal the previous evening. I cannot remember how many times I practiced those words: they were, "I'll just roll my eyelashes like this", of course flicking my eyelids and rolling my eyes as I spoke. Funny as I was at the dress rehearsal I just was not going to perform that evening. The full meaning of my teacher's order to take home the costume did not penetrate until that evening when my mother was helping me to get dressed and combing my hair. How am I to walk this long distance from home to the Theatre donned in this long dress? My father was ready. I was not. Ward Theatre or no Ward Theatre I was not going to walk from Beeston Street to the Theatre.

The Ward Theatre, located in the heart of downtown Kingston, was to Jamaica, what Carnegie Hall is to New York in the U.S.A. This was the place where many actors performed. If you were in acting and you did not perform at the Ward Theatre then you were not "saying a thing". The fact that my schoolmates and I would be performing at the Ward made us instant celebrities.

I was fully decked out in the long dress. I started to "bawl". There was snot coming out of my nose and water running from every orifice on the front of my face. Suddenly my body was stricken with a compelling sensation as if the other orifices on my body would soon join in the medley. My belly was rolling as I tried hard not to let the crescendo burst forth. I stood shivering. Bottled inside of me was the desire to express to my father my fear and trepidation, but I did not know how. I just did not know how. Would I suffer for stating my feelings? Neither of my parents ever used corporal punishment on me up to that point, but I just kept reading the austere look on my father's face and did not know what this look meant.

All this time my father did not have a clue that one of his little girls was having a panic attack. After all, in those days, children were expected to be compliant and there was no Super Nanny to buffer parental anxiety. Should you need such an intervention your super nanny would be a whipping on the behind. At the age of seven, I learned quickly what protocol was and what it was not. I learned well from my older cousins in the country. You see, I dare not tell my father that I was not going to perform this evening or that I was afraid to walk on the street with this long dress. What! Afraid? After all fear is nonexistent in the character of the Ashanti and Samuel said I am the descendant of Ashanti Africans. I am an Ashanti.

Anyhow, knowing my father there was no room for me to have my way. There would definitely be no negotiations or debate. This was unthinkable! If you took time out to contemplate, the predicament that I was in, you would really begin to wonder what the reason was for all the noise and tears. What was my fear? Was it the distance from our home to the Theatre? After all, I realize now that the entire walk from home to the Theatre was not as far as it seemed so many years ago.

Ward Theatre was close to the school that I attended at that time. Besides, I had traveled that route every day on my way to and from school. Somehow, as I age and return to some of the places where I grew up as a child, they take on a different visual perspective. The Ward Theatre was only a short distance away from St. Joseph's Infant School that was located on Duke Street. My sister, my Chinese friend from across the street and I, traveled together at least twice daily to and from school. Sometimes the trip was four times for the day. Those were the days when lunch money was not available so we walked home for lunch. It was okay for me to be seen walking home to and from school.

What provided this level of comfort for me at that time? It was precisely because I was dressed in uniform like every other schoolchild. The nosey people along the way did not ask any questions because it was obvious I was on my way to school.

I was one of "Bah Sam's" children on her way to school. What then was the problem on that day in the summer of 1949? I was preoccupied with the thought of what people would be thinking about me. I began to imagine people, as they would stop to question my father along the way. My father was like the Mayor of Beeston Street, from Wildman Street to Duke Street. I envision people asking questions and my proud Maroon father stopping to oblige with the answer. I never in my wildest dreams thought of such a time as this while in the Country, Accompong Maroon Town.

One day I am in the country and another day I am in this busy place called Town (short for Kingston). In the country, I had the freedom of walking barefooted on the slippery muddy stones and playing outdoors with my cousins. Six months ago, I was living in Accompong Town with Aunt Betsy. Since the age of three my sister Una and I lived with her, only returning to Kingston for the summer holidays. I had many experiences with my Aunt Betsy, Uncle Vernal and Sister Mac. When all three of them came to town, our home was bombarded with prayers, singing and praying in "tongues". Uncle Vernal never prayed aloud or prayed for a long time. He was more subdued when in the spirit. Samuel never interrupted their worship no matter what was their style. The routine of us visiting the country continued until one week-end before

Christmas, we were back in Town and going to St. Josephs' Infant School in Kingston.

My education started in Accompong Maroon Town and my teacher was a Mr. Frazier. I was born "under the clock". In Jamaica this is an expression used to describe a person who was born in Kingston. The exact place of my birth was at the Victoria Jubilee Lying-In Hospital in Kingston. How then did we end up living in Accompong? My father believed that the best way for us to learn and know our rich African history, heritage and culture was to live it. Because of his deep-rooted connection and belief in our ancestral legacy, he sent my sister Una and me to live in Accompong and to attend the School there. He knew that the value of a good education was priceless. Money could not buy what we would experience if we lived in Accompong. He was proud to say that the teachers in Accompong were the best. After all, he was a by-product of the School in Accompong.

Our education would be twofold: based on Samuel's curriculum design, the academics would be given by our Schoolteacher and our culture from our elders. He believed that this experience was going to offer us a better understanding of our African ancestors and whom we are as a people. Most country folk in those days yearned to live in Kingston, and still do. My mother was not thrilled with the idea of us going to live in the Country; however, I do not remember any confrontation about the matter between my father and her.

My father was educated in Accompong Maroon Town and believed in the quality of their primary education. Nelson Mandela said, "Education is the most powerful weapon which you can use to change the world." Although Samuel was before Mandela's time, he also believed this. He wanted his children to have the best education and learn about our ancestors at the same time.

At that time the elders would tell us one story over and over again. The central theme of this story was a story about our ancestors who fought with determination to keep their freedom. It was a story about the unity of the ancestors and commitment to one agenda, freedom. It was about the War the British lost. Yes, a war the British lost to my African ancestors from Ghana.

Samuel stood and reached for his "dress up" felt hat. He had two felt hats and a bowl hat. One felt hat he wore to work, the other he would dress in and the bowl hat he wore when he went to watch cricket at Sabina Park. Oh, boy he was ready! My father was dressed in his dark suit and tie and he was wearing his "dress up" felt hat. He was placing his upper gold teeth in position with his tongue. The upper denture was loose and with this procedure with his tongue, he managed to eat and talk with the loose denture with much ease. I looked over at my father and gazed at him, this time my eyes made contact with his. For the first time since the drama began this evening. I was mesmerized by the expression on his face. He was ready, not angry.

Now after all this anxiety, I finally realized that it was "safe" for me to speak to my father. I did not know what to say to him and how to say it. I was tongue-tied. I only know that the time was safe for me to unfreeze, let go of my fears and tension and stop the "bawling". I guess my father felt my pain and fear because being the wise man he was he spoke first. "Are you ready?" he said. Fancy him asking me that question. A man on a wild riding horse could see that I was ready. I was not quick to reply, however, I was direct with my answer.

I can barely remember what I said to him or how I said it. I know the message went across to him that I did not want to wear the costume on the street. I blurted out something that was enough for my father to understand my agony. As soon as the words of my response were blurted out, I froze. I began to anticipate, what his reaction would be. I could not even say what I was anticipating. To me his next move was unpredictable. I cannot give an analysis of the communication that ensued between us. I just know that from the look in his eyes, he understood my message. He saw my fear. Somehow, he came to know that the problem was the long dress; that I did not want to wear this long dress on the street.

To my amazement, my father said nothing. He did not hesitate. He took his handkerchief from his pant pocket and wiped the snot from my face. Then he placed the handkerchief in his pocket, secured his hat on his head, bent over and picked me up. He placed me in his arms and started to walk out the door. He executed this gesture with such precision that I became frightened and did not know what to do or say. Now, I was just heaving a little, no rapid chest movement, not even a tear. I knew then that this was my moment. This would be the anchor for all that was to come. The events that led to this moment opened a sort of capsule that was around me and out burst the spirits of the old to shape and nurture the spirit of young.

It was a climax and a beginning for me at the same time. It was a moment so sharp and profound that the impact still hangs in my spirit today. It was my moment, my beginning. Many questions raced through my mind at that moment in time. My! My father was strong. Was my father planning to carry me all the way to the theatre? How far would he go with me in his hand? Was he going to take me down the street? All these questions were short lived. The grip of my father's arms, the feel of his strong body, and the sense of purpose in his every step, all helped to cement in my mind the Maroon ethos. I was embarrassed for my father; but more so for myself. Many issues of the day then some sixty plus years ago was the catalyst for embarrassment; my wearing of this long dress on the street was one of them.

The dress was made from a bright orange-yellow cotton floral print fabric. The orange-yellow flowers crowded the material in such a way that the material seemed to be orange-yellow. The dress was one piece with the blouse attached to the skirt and a streamer on each side of the blouse. The neck was round, opened at the back and finished with piping and a hook and eye to fasten at the back. Large full sleeves that we called puffed sleeves complimented the blouse. The floor length skirt of the dress was gathered at the waist. This costume's, puffed sleeves, full long skirt and ribbons, all added to the floral garden effect of my attire. I felt like a fool.

Nevertheless, nothing seemed to interfere with his purpose. Samuel's mission was to see me complete my purpose for that day. His action on that day had kept me inexplicably connected to the spirit of my Ashanti African ancestors the Maroons. What was more profound was the igniting of our spirits, his, mine and our ancestors. It is difficult to explain. I knew then that my father would always be there for me. For us.

It seems to me that my African ancestors possessed this innate quality to nurture and to groom. It seems to me to be a quality that contradicts a character of being wild. How else could they have developed people of such enviable character? I know that something special happened to me at that moment. My father demonstrated to me his ability to solve a problem almost instantaneously. Without dialogue, he helped me connect with his ability to turn a problem into an opportunity. This was his moment to show to us that he would be there for us. It was this personal sense of ownership that had us referring to our father as "mi daddy". Samuel made each of us feel as if he was our personal possession. He was mine as much as he was my sister's father.

Everything happened so sudden that evening. I was in shock. From the look on my mother's face, I believe she was also in shock. She could not understand what was going on. My father strutted carefully. He was really going to carry me.

My father was five feet five inches tall, very strong and very muscular. He was not "pumping iron" but his muscles sure were firm. This shows how naturally strong my ancestors were. He developed his physique from a young boy. He had to farm provisions. His farm is still at Old Town in Accompong. The area is overgrown as no one farms in that area now. Old Town was previously known as Ann-feri Town. Today huge breadfruit trees and other plants are among the foliage in that area. Old Town is the site of Kojo's and Nanny's burial place. Kojo and the older generations first settled in Old Town until, the area was flooded and became water logged. The residents therefore moved to higher ground. Samuel also described a place in Accompong with quick sand. I have asked some of the older people but so far, no one can identify such a place.

Samuel held me securely in his arms. I grabbed him around his neck with both my arms and buried my face in his neck, all the time I hid my face from the public's view. My father stepped boldly and confidently on his way to the Theatre. I maintained this position with my face buried in his neck until we arrived at The Ward. I was so entrapped in my little world of embarrassment that I could not recall what happened when we arrived at the Theatre.

Fast forward with me if you will to 1978 and overseas, I remember this incident when I transported my second son to school on the first day of Junior High. My son crouched on the back seat of my car and stayed in that position because he did not want his classmates to see him being taken to school in a car. He was embarrassed because when you are in Junior High you are not taken to school in a car unless of course you are driving. You travel by bus or walk to school. The mode of travel for them at that age was a symbol of maturity and I was about to blow his cover and render him to his peers as an immature lad. My position then was what, a motorcar! A luxury I never had until I was a young adult.

With my father's every step, I felt his strong character and spirit of determination, commitment and confidence. I was somewhat short in stature, still short, so I was easy to carry. I am not sure how much I weighed then, but I am sure that whatever my weight was, my father would still have carried me. As young as I was, I could feel my father's energy as he carried me. His energy gave me a sense of security and trust. I knew I was safe in my father's arms. It was an energy that transformed me from a fearful hollering child into a tempered human being. His hold on me was firm and strong. It was a hold that was devoid of all the characteristics that could be used to depict him as being a wild, ferocious untamed warrior, the description given to my ancestors by the British colonialist. A description that lingers to this day.

From the moment that my father picked me up, something ignited inside my spirit and provided a life connection with the spirit of my father. He demonstrated to me that he was a no-nonsense person who would find a way to do what had to be done, if he believed it was the right thing to do. His decision to carry me that day reminds me of the many stories that he told me about his hero and heroine, Kojo and Nanny.

Samuel must have been sizing up all that I was going through during the preparation for the theatre. How many times did he witness my mother comb my hair, preparing me for school or church? This was not the first time that my mother did this task. I want to believe that what seemed like a genuine delay was to him a genuine camouflage. What was he thinking all this time?

I tell this story about the happenings on that eventful day; when my father picked me up in his arms to carry me to perform at Ward Theatre, as part of my prelude to a script that will tell about my African ancestors, and freedom fighters the Maroons. I return to this event because this "moment" forms the anchor and frames my life's experience with my father. It continually reconnects me to the quest of my ancestors as they fought to protect their freedom in the Cockpit Mountains and other areas in Jamaica.

My father's action on that day still resounds with me as I travel this journey called living. No other event has made such an impact on my life. I believe that every now and then, an event happens in one's life and that event leaves a mark that anchors all of life's' other events. As I am taken back to the events of that evening, I experience a new birth, a new dimension of the spirit of the Ashanti African man, my father Samuel Nathaniel Rowe. I cannot help but feel a revived energy as my spirit is recharged. It is more than a hair raising or goose pimple experience. It is as if some magnetic pull suddenly draws me to a place or state where I connect with the spirit of my father and my ancestors. It is hard to explain; however, it is real. This event continues to infuse me with some sort of spiritual karma that opens the bloodline and reconnects me to the spirit of my father and our ancestors. That infusion continues to provide a life stream for me to this day. It is a stream that has shaped my character, defined my purpose and strengthens my desire to learn more about my ancestors.

I was blessed to feel the soul and share in a depth of spiritual transformation. It is within the framework of this experience that I latched onto the meaning and significance of my African ancestors. This was my moment.

3

THE WRONG MARK

The stereotyping of my African ancestors and me continues today. Maroons, as we are still called, are not supposed to be real people. To this day, there remains a distant mythical association with the people known as Maroons. My father tells stories of how others depicted us as some type of wild deranged specie that was transported from Africa during the Atlantic Slave Trade. My father's mission was to dispel all the negative portrayals that were told about the Maroons. Samuel spent his life showing us how brave and resourceful our ancestors were. It was in the Cockpit Mountains of Jamaica that my ancestors were compelled to fight for their life, their identity, and to remain free. People in Jamaica and abroad continue to believe that the name Maroon, given to my ancestors by the British, was a name that truly depicted the person and character of a breed of Africans called "Maroons". You see, how else one would understand the humanity of a people who for years have been labeled wild and given all sorts of descriptions by others alien to our experience. Maroons like to be recognized as a brave people.

4

SAMUEL, THE PERSON

My father, Samuel Nathaniel Rowe, was the second child of James and Jane Rowe. My father was born August 1898, in Accompong Nanny Town, as the place was then called. His birth was one hundred and sixty years after the signing of the Peace Treaty between Captain Kojo and the British colonials Saddler and Guthrie on March 1, 1738. The Windward Treaty was signed later in 1739. Samuel, his brothers and sisters were descendant of Kojo. These descendants were the first Africans in the Western Hemisphere who fought for and won their freedom. Other Africans in Jamaica were emancipated one hundred years later, 1838. Samuel and his ancestors were people of great faith and determination. Theirs was a determination never to be enslaved again after being released by their Spanish slave owners. It was this determination to keep their freedom at all cost, which kept them at war with the British for over eighty years.

Their artistry, resilience, determination and wit may have been what earned them the name: Maroons, the wild ones.

There are people in Jamaica who believe that the people that are known as Maroons are different from Jamaicans in other parts of the country. Some Jamaicans still believe that Maroons are wild, ferocious people and our eyes are red. Some including Jamaicans even believe that a life threatening science surrounds the Maroons hence, their ability to ward off evil and communicate with the dead to carry out some act of evil.

Samuel wanted to erase these misconceptions and expose us to his truth. I know that my father, my aunts and uncles who lived in Accompong all had a spiritual connection with our ancestors. I never knew them to communicate with any dead. I know however that they were very sensitive to the presence of the spirits of our ancestors.

My father always had a bottle of rum in the house. I recall that sometimes when we sat at the table to eat he would sprinkle a little rum on the floor and mutter something. It was as if he sensed the presence of someone or something. I never questioned his action neither was I afraid during those encounters. This was not a daily ritual. I therefore believe he was responding to the spiritual presence of our ancestors.

My father's face was oval; his head was round and cropped with fine, black, soft, curly, wooly hair. His hair was a mix of Indian and African or what we have come to know as "bad hair". Twice, I had the opportunity to run my fingers through his hair, once as he laid his head on my lap at the doctor's office and the other time as he lay dying. There was no male pattern baldness and no alopecia. He kept his hair short at all times, and visited the barber, his brother Israel, at least every two weeks.

His forehead was round; His eyebrows were thick and shapely; eyes were sleepy with upper eyelids that had a slight bulge at the outer corners, a pudgy nose neatly centered and large but shapely lips; especially the lower lip. His cheeks were soft and swept slightly upward towards some big ears. His face was always clean, thanks to his daily shaving routine. He would mix a lather of soap and water with his shaving brush. He then applied the lather to cover his temples, cheeks, upper lip around his mouth chin and neck. He used a very sharp razor to remove the lather and hair from his face. He could almost do this with his eyes closed. His body was well proportioned with a torso that would be the envy of today's "potbelly" young men, and his behind was pleasing to look at, not big and not high. He had a good physique.

I never saw him naked so my description is with him clothed in his boxer underpants. Yes, he wore his boxers to the sea. In those days, the boxer was called drawers more so than it is now. His hands were huge for his size and his fingers were short and thick. When he made a fist, you were looking at a round object that was the size of a large orange.

He never told me the size of his shoes but I now imagine he wore a size nine. Samuel had a commanding attitude and a posture that accentuated his stance. He walked with his shoulders thrown back and his every step was as precise as a soldier who was on a marching parade. I later learned that the drill sergeant was never absent and was his God. Samuel drilled into us that our physical attributes must never be a deterrent to our innate capabilities.

Let us face it; we had no one to perform a nose job and no bleaching cream. Even if there was, Samuel drilled into us the importance of accepting our physical attributes. We were blessed to self-administer facials with natural herbs and plants. The most famous was the tuna scrub. I am five feet tall or short. Samuel left me to feel like a giant.

A few weeks ago, I was talking with a 7th Grade student. We stood in front of each other and I was able to look him directly in his eyes. It was the first time that I really connected with the fact that I am vertically challenged. I was amused. It was at that time that I recalled how on several occasions after meeting someone in person after many conversations on the telephone, the individual would be very surprised at my height.

Samuel taught me not to waste time on the challenges of life nor my physical attributes; not the length nor texture of my hair or at the colour of my skin. These, he said, were self imposed limitations and obstacles. He taught us how to ride the wave of time and not to strangle our success by self-imposed obstacles. I believe he nurtured us in this manner because he understood the stigma in Jamaica that is associated with being a Maroon. A Maroon has two strikes, one being black and the other being a Maroon.

Samuel did not allow us to socialize with our neighbours; so outdoor play in Kingston was limited to the other children who lived in our tenement. We would watch for him coming home. One of us was the lookout person. That person would signal as soon as she saw the sharp seams from his khaki pants. You could see his stride before you saw his face. We would all run indoors and start to read or do schoolwork.

Today I sometimes feel that Samuel knew what we were up to. He was always prim and proper even in his diction. My sister Millie tells me that she remembers that the first big word she heard as a child came from our father. She cannot recall what sparked the outburst but our father called us "unscrupulous". He always said what was on his mind. You need not guess at his ability to articulate exactly what he was thinking. Samuel never minced his words. He mastered the art of verbalize without meditating on the sharpness of his words.

I remember once my mother was about to take us someplace so without hesitating she said, "a ready you ready aready". My father promptly and endearingly said, "No Rene", as he affectionately called her, "Not a ready you ready aready, are you ready to go?" He was comfortable to deliver his message as long as in his opinion his words represented the truth. He made no apology to the hearer and he was precise in his delivery. It was for this reason that at my wedding, I asked my "Uncle Ivan" to respond on behalf of the Bride's father. The custom then at a wedding reception was for the father of the Bride to say something on behalf of his daughter. I have an enormous respect and love for my daddy. The difficulty at my wedding day however, was my uncertainty and inability to predict the content of Samuel's speech. Since that day in 1949 when he picked me up and carried me, I was never sure what to expect from him. I certainly was not open for any embarrassment, not on my wedding day. He was not fond of my husband; however, he respected my choice of a mate. He was careful to outline to me my wifely duties and the things I should not do such as go into a man's pocket. That instruction was delivered to me with such authority that to this day a feeling of betrayal overshadows me each time I am tempted to search my husband's pocket. Anytime I do something contrary to my father's authoritative teaching, I feel like a convicted sinner.

My father had a remarkable sense of humor. I remember dinnertime on a Sunday afternoon as special. I believe this is so in most Jamaican families. The menu was predictable. My mother was able to secure a pineapple as the fruit to be served after dinner. She too was resourceful and wasted nothing. It is simple to make pineapple juice. She peeled the pineapple, washed the peel, added a few pieces of fresh ginger, and covered this with cold water. This mixture was then boiled for about fifteen minutes, removed from the fire and left to cool. When the mixture was cool, she added sugar to sweeten the juice and poured the drink into a juice jug.

We never seemed to have enough ice to cool the drink. We owned a small refrigerator and therefore ice was never in abundance. Ice was purchased from the iceman. My mother used an ice pick to break the ice into small pieces. She then added the chopped ice to the pine mixture. The warm Jamaican temperature was always successful in competing for the cool of the ice. We watched the beads of water gently roll down the side of the juice jar. Soon the jar was sitting in water that was cooler than the juice.

Samuel poured us some pine juice, poured himself some and retorted, "Every Sunday we have to drink pine tea." Samuel's intent was to draw attention to the fact that we must know when to change. After his remark about the warm pine drink, we all laughed, including my mother. Samuel's face was straight. He showed no emotion. We knew that he was laughing inside. That was the last day we were served "pine tea". Like his African ancestors, Samuel did not seek popularity. His intentions were centered on a central theme of the Maroon practice to speak the truth.

Samuel represented the epitome of an unyielding spirit, resolute decency, a strong character, self-esteem and will. He fathered four children , all of whom were girls. He coached us how to be independent women, how to respect ourselves, respect others and fight for our rights. For him, the African lifestyle was the central cord to the development of our persona.

As a child, I never quite understood his stance and demeanor. Being a Maroon to Samuel was more than words, it was a way of life. Maroons spent much time praying, loving and sharing with each other. This was the practice among the older Maroons. Samuel was a devout believer in the Christian doctrine and followed closely the tradition of his ancestors in his walk and worship of God Almighty. He was not in church all the time. I remember that at one time he attended the Moravian Church at the corner of North Street and Duke Street in Kingston.

He was a man who used his knowledge of the word of God to guide and mold our character. Samuel read his Bible continuously. I watched him often and knew when he was meditating, praying for his family, and us and praying for Jamaica. He read much from the Psalms, Proverbs and The New Testament. His constant prayer was that he would live to see us "pass the worst". He deliberately verbalized this desire very often. I was not happy with his request. I wanted Samuel to live a long life. I wanted him to see my accomplishment and to serve him. His spiritual life was not a show. He did not own a "Sunday best". He was always dressed immaculately whether he was at work or at home. He held no position in any religious denomination nor was he a member of any. He had his special period of worship on Sunday afternoons. Our modest living room provided the sanctuary and his pew was his favourite rocking chair.

This place was set aside for Samuel. We did not question his ownership of this space on Sunday or any other day. The preacher he listened to was constant. Every Sunday evening it was Billy Graham and the sermon was heard through the airwaves of our Telefunken radio. Samuel had the volume of the radio loud enough for the sound to envelope the entire house yet not disturb anyone. This was not difficult since the house at Beeston Street was three rooms. This practice continued also when we moved to Duhaney Park. Samuel had his Bible and joined the young Billy Graham in the reading of the scripture. We knew Billy Graham's signature hymn, *"Just as I am without one plea..."* Samuel joined his radio community in singing this song. He belted out the words of the song as if his breath of life hinged on every syllable and every note. He sang as if he was the assigned soloist at every session; and the musical accompaniment was from a piped organ in the room.

We knew that the neighbours heard it all. Samuel cared little about their thoughts of him. He knew that he was not being a nuisance. He sang as if he was making a personal statement to God Almighty and every moment ushered him closer in the presence of his God.

I never interrupted him when he is in this posture. Sometimes I sat at the dining table and listened. My sisters did not even stay in his presence. There was something different about his calm and apparent detachment from what was happening around him. I knew he was still connected with our activities; however, he was not distracted from his spiritual devotion. Somehow as I watched him, I too, felt the energy in the voice of Billy Graham. I heard his overt denunciation of sin, experienced his compelling appeal to the sinner and connected with his love for his God, God's love for man and Billy's love for the people. Like his African ancestors, Samuel recognized in Billy Graham the fearless spirit of a young man who stood for what he believed; a young man who cared nothing about being politically correct.

This was another opportunity for me to understand the spirit of my African ancestors. They had the Spirit of God and embraced the spirit of truth. Samuel taught me what it means to be silent and how to enter in the presence of God. His African ancestors were spiritual people who patterned living according to the precepts of the bible. Their success and their living were fortified by their faith in a supreme being and a determination to walk the high road to spirituality, morality and truth.

My African ancestors were honest hardworking people. Maroons were not beggars. They transferred this legacy to our generation. It did not matter to Samuel that he placed us in the Catholic Church. He shared with us later that the Roman Catholics have the resources that we need for personal growth. He was concerned with our development as humans and our application of our spirituality. He wanted to be sure that we understood the spirituality within us and that we made a commitment to serve God unconditionally.

He introduced us to a God who had no boundaries, whose power was beyond the confines of a denomination, who loved unconditionally, who was compassionate and full of mercy and grace. Samuel taught us that the colour of a man's skin did not dictate his ability to love and show the love of God, a love according to my daddy was an all-inclusive love. He was concerned with the irresponsible behavior of some men. Samuel did not father a son; had no extramarital affair and spent his life coaching us about the spirit of independence.

We saw daddy give. Even when he had nothing, he always found "something" to give. Sometimes it was his advice, his encouragement, maybe a smile, or a listening ear. Samuel taught us how to give. His sister V otherwise known as Aunt V was also a giver. I call her the Harriet Tubman of Accompong. Many of my cousins living overseas especially in England, sojourned with either Samuel or Aunt V in Kingston prior to migrating overseas. Some are still living in Kingston to this day.

Samuel and Aunt V pioneered and developed the "Immigration Transition Training Academy for Accompong Maroons" (ITTAAM). It was at this Training Academy that many Accompong participants received information on acculturation into a society outside of Accompong, a society that may be as close as Kingston. Their Academy was fashioned on the syllabus of experiential learning. The lecturers were Samuel, his sister V and her son Ivan. These lecturers were serious. Uncle Ivan was a Soldier in the British Air Force and fought in World War Two. He was very stern and disciplined.

Students from the country had to first master the skill of speaking clearly. Language Arts was a must. I remember him giving my cousin the proper pronunciation for words. It was breakfast, lunch or dinner not "bickle". It was morning and not "mawning". They were instructed to give the directions to the bus stop and travel from home to parade.

Parade was the central point.

Security was an important aspect so they were taken to the central police station and were given the rules of safety. Strangers were just that "STRANGERS". They were not people to be embraced. Treat them well, a quick "how de do" and move on. This was until you get to know them better. Reading was important so they had to be able to tell what the topical issues in the Gleaner were. Dress code was also important. The girls were given instruction on how to dress. The length of the skirt had to be below the knees.

As a young boy, my father lived in Accompong Maroon Town at a place known as Hill Top. He lived with his father James his sisters and other brothers. His mother died when he was a young boy. He understood the value of the legacy of the land bequeath to us by our ancestors. As a youngster, Samuel would farm the land, and helped with household chores. What is that? These included a walk to Joney's Tavern or "Junitavan", a distance of half a mile, to fetch water every morning, pull fire stick for cooking, milk the goats and move the animals.

His sister Betsy was the matriarch of the family and cared for the other children after their mother died. The family did not raise more than two pigs at a time. Whatever was cultivated was mainly for household use. During the hunting season, they would hunt for baldpate and other birds. These made good roasting delicacies. Some ground produce was prepared for sale at the market.

I am sure that other children in the rural areas of Jamaica must have similar experiences. What makes this information of importance is to know that "Maroons" also lived as most others in the rural parts of Jamaica.

Samuel soon realized that economic independence was central to the ability to experience full independence. For this reason, he started to explore avenues for economic freedom outside Accompong. His dream was to be able to care for his family as the elders and men of Accompong did for theirs.

Before we were born, Samuel traveled to Cuba on two occasions to do farm work. He told us he "was looking for a way to support us." He said the "man is supposed to take care of his family." He would say, "I just want to be able to provide and live to see you all pass the worst." Although Kojo, Nanny and the other Ashanti Africans had secured valuable land and their sovereignty, they lacked the capital to develop their resources. This lack of financial capital did not prevent my ancestors from entry to the marketplace. Their commodities came from within their natural resources, mainly ground provision. My ancestors worked hard to eke out an existence from the natural resources of the Cockpit Mountains. Samuel tried to follow the pattern of his ancestors including his father. He soon realized that this life in Cuba was not for him. He was passionate about his Maroon heritage and spent his life living the ideals and emulating the characteristics of his heroine and hero, Nanny and Kojo; characteristics of bravery, spirituality and determination.

His was a fearless life buffeted by a respect for all and the discipline to execute his convictions. Samuel was for freedom and equity for all, but not necessarily anti-establishment. He understood Nanny's and Kojo's fight to maintain freedom and spent his life articulating these values and characteristics to us, his four daughters.

Like his ancestors, he spent time to analyze any situation on hand. One thing I learned from my father is that my Ashanti African ancestors spent valued time planning. At the time of the struggle for freedom, my ancestors would plan the activity and strategy for the next day. Tomorrow's activities would be debated, tried, and mapped out and ended with a contingency plan. My ancestors were visionaries. I am not sure how much of these traits are genetic. I do know that Samuel spent time to beat the ideas of planning and decision making into our heads.

Samuel's favourite saying to us was, "never say 'if I did know' after the fact, and try to say 'if I did know' before the fact." This instruction from my father was simple, but had a profound connection to the importance of planning, especially anticipatory planning. When we plan, we must ask of the Holy Spirit within us, "what if"? What will be the consequence of putting this plan into action?

He told us of Marcus Garvey and felt pity for Jamaicans who could only see the boat to Africa and not the message for us all. Listen for guidance then choose to be obedient with the follow through. In other words, make the right choice. In today's vernacular, be proactive. My Ashanti African ancestors demonstrated their ability to use anticipatory planning. How else could they fight for over eighty years to remain free from the attacks of the British? Later in the text, I will talk about the war in detail. I will talk about Samuel and his plans for economic freedom.

Samuel was not afraid to change his mind and as a result, he returned to Jamaica to try the local job market after two seasons of living and working in Cuba. He did not return with any liquid asset but he definitely came back with a wealth of intellectual capital. He was speaking Spanish fluently. My sisters and I listened to him speak Spanish with his Cuban friend Paul who was an ex-boxer who lived nearby our home. Paul had to pass our home to get to his, and our gate was necessary stop for him every evening. Samuel and Paul had these long conversations, all the time speaking in Spanish. The exchange of words, gesticulations, facial expressions and the tone of their voices were enough for me to understand when it had been a good day at work for either man.

Under Samuel's tutelage my sister and I mastered the ability to count, tell the time of day, tell our age, say where we were born, and say the days of the week and the months of the year in Spanish. We could ask for water or bread in Spanish language. In his African language, he told us that "abinaqua" was a non-Maroon and "aborno" was a white man. "Nigger" he said was the name given to a non-maroon who entered our community. Again, I saw the determination of an Ashanti African who was not willing to give up on the mission at hand, while he was teaching us how to speak Spanish, the language of our ancestors, and the importance of perseverance. It was Samuel's ability to speak Spanish fluently that opened the opportunity for him to get a job with Abe Issa at Issa store on King Street in Kingston. Samuel was hired, he told us, as a "floor walker". His marriage certificate lists his occupation as "Shop Assistant". Before my sister Una was born in 1940, he was a Spanish interpreter at one of the most prestigious stores in Jamaica. He could also speak the African language. At that time, store managers and cashiers had to be of the lighter complexion. He was not.

One thing I know was that my father made me very proud of him at all times. He showed us how to value our person and not to use physical features or characteristics as a guideline to judge anyone's' character or ability. His point of character reference was always that of our ancestors. I remember visiting him at Issa on my way from school, Immaculate Conception High School. When I visited that day, Samuel was surprised. My visit was not announced. As soon as he saw me he had a proud look on his face, he threw back his shoulders and displayed that all familiar smile that I had come to know. It was a smile of success. He then spent time to show me to all his co-workers. This was his opportunity to present his offspring to his peers. Samuel also worked at Myrtle Bank, a hotel owned by Issa. Myrtle Bank was located not far from Issa store. Samuel was the packer of goods for transport overseas. He was proud of the fact that not one item was broken during transport from Jamaica to places across the seas.

I remember the year that my sister and I returned from Accompong to live in Kingston. It was shortly after the New Year and my father came home to tell my mother that he was going to work for a few days in St. Mary with Abe Issa at Issas' new hotel, "Tower Isle". I was six years old at the time. I remember my father being away from home for a week. My father was very important to Abe Issa's empire. When he returned from Tower Isle, he had several stories to tell about the visitors and how Issa felt good about this powerful Spanish speaking Maroon. Samuel said, "Issa introduced me to the visitors. I was the interpreter. You should see me sitting with the Spanish people." As far as Samuel was concerned, his ancestors earned the status to be recognized even before their capture from Africa.

My sisters and I were beneficiaries of Samuel's employment with Issa. My mother was given the best materials, taffeta, cotton prints and silk to make dresses for us. My mother however was not a dressmaker by any stretch of one's imagination. The sleeves would suffer because of her inability to construct a dress free hand. To complete a fit she would "splice" the sleeves. This meant that she had to insert a piece of fabric to make the sleeve fit. My father was upset but said nothing. He was upset because she had enough material to make the sleeve with a single cut. We also wore the best shoes available. Samuel remained loyal to Abe Issa and continued to work there for years.

My father was always quick to drive home to us the importance of giving respect to get respect. Many times too numerous to remember, Samuel would tell us and demonstrate to us the importance of looking someone in the eye when talking to them. He told us not to look to the ground and rub our toes in the dirt while talking to the white skinned man nor any person for that matter. He mirrored our behaviour as an example of what not to do; curving his shoulders forward, bending his head while looking to the ground, and rubbing the front of his right toes in the ground as if to put out a cigarette butt. This behavior to him was inappropriate and did not show character, certainly not the character of our African ancestors.

I vividly remember a real life demonstration of this rule by him when I attended St. Joseph's Girls School. Yours truly took an exam for a scholarship. The scholarship was the ticket for me to enter this prestigious High School called Immaculate Conception High School. I passed the scholarship exam; however, the headmistress of St. Joseph's Girls School at that time thought it was prudent to award the scholarship to a Chinese girl. I went home and told my father what had happened. Sure enough, the following morning Samuel went to see the headmistress. The Headmistress was a nun of the Franciscan Order. I was nervous knowing that my father was not going to be easy with this woman. She was Caucasian with blue eyes and she was taller than he was. The words respect and discipline, started to echo in my mind. My father and I were escorted to the headmistresses' office.

We stood and waited for her to beckon us to sit. He spoke first. Samuel looked the Headmistress in her eyes and asked her, "Why are you taking away the scholarship from Norma? She won that scholarship and worked hard for it." I was being denied the scholarship that I worked hard to get and the headmistress was going to award the scholarship to another girl. I do not believe that my father cared whether the other girl was pink, blue, black or gold. As far as he was concerned, it was the principle of the deal that mattered. The headmistress flatly told him that I was younger than the other girl was and that she would give me the scholarship the following year. Samuel looked her in her blue eyes and said, "What happens if you are not here next year? Norma won the scholarship to attend Immaculate now, so you will give it to her now." I started Immaculate Conception High School that year in 1957.

Once again, I came to grips with the spirit and character of my African Maroon father. He was direct with his demand. He was taking a stand for what he knew was my right. Nothing about his disposition would justify him being called wild or untamed. As far as he was concerned, he was an African talking with a woman of Caucasian descent. It did not matter that she was a nun. He must have seen beyond the black veil that covered her head, beyond the long thick dark brown dress with long sleeves and the starched round bib that covered her chest. He saw what I could not see then and he fought. He was raised by the lessons of our African ancestors and leaders Kojo and Nanny. My father knew that St. Joseph's Girls School was the feeder school for Immaculate Conception High School. He also knew that he would have some difficulty finding my tuition for this prestigious High School. Abe Issa told my father to prepare me for the scholarship exam. I remember that before I started to attend Immaculate, my father took me to visit Abe Issa at his home then on South Camp Road. Mr. Issa shook my hand, congratulated me, and told me how invaluable my father was to his establishment.

During the first year at Immaculate, my grades started to fall. This bright little girl was failing. I would lose the scholarship if my grades were low. That was a condition to keep the scholarship. Being the keen administrator he was, he decided some management systems in the home had to change. I was responsible for cooking the dinner because I was home from school before the others. This was additional to my other responsibilities in the home. Samuel immediately had to do something about my failing grades.

He called a family meeting as is typical of his ancestors. Ashanti custom is "One man can't rule." He outlined the problem to my sisters and at the same time gave them his decision. "Norma is failing her work and we must help her. We can't let her fail. You all will share her work in the home." My sisters were not happy. There was no room for discussion. We were going to do everything necessary together as a family to improve my grades. My father showed us how to take full responsibility for our actions. We made no excuse. We did not debate. We worked together and spent time on the solution. Failure was not an acceptable outcome and any excuse was intolerable. My sisters were not happy because they felt I was escaping my responsibility and chores. I graduated from Immaculate Conception High School in June 1960 with six subjects including Math, English and Biology.

Samuel wanted us to be independent. He was our coach in this life's journey. His decision was to share all that he knew and pass on to us as many skills as was possible. One such skill of his was swimming. He was determined to make swimmers out of us. Samuel would take us to Gold Street pier every Sunday morning. He would dunk us in the cold icy water. I was afraid; my sister was afraid. Samuel swam like a fish. He tried to help us to stand in the water but the waves had more control over our little bodies and kept us doing a dance through the cold salty water. The stones at the bottom of the water were also cold, slippery and sometimes rough. There was no white sand at the Gold Street Pier no sand at all. We were not the only persons at the Pier. It seems that the pier was the beach for some Kingstonians. One minute Samuel held our hands and would show us how to go underwater and the next minute he let us go and he was off under the water like a fish. My sister and I never mastered the art of swimming. We were scared for him and for ourselves. Even though others around us were enjoying themselves my sister and I were scared.

Samuel loved cricket and cycle sports. He spent Friday evenings at

Race Course, now known as George VI Park, enjoying the bicyclists competition. He never owned a bicycle neither did he believe that we should learn how to ride a cycle. He said such an activity was not ladylike. I never understood why he said this.

Samuel took us to several cricket matches at Sabina Park. He spent valuable time to teach us the sport. He told us how the bowler sets the field for each pitch of the ball. This was serious strategy. There was the fast bowler, and others. Each place on the field was set to get the batsman out. There was slip, country, cover, extra cover, square leg, fine leg, backward short leg, short leg, mid on, mid off, and silly mid-on: this one required immediate explanation as to why it was called "silly mid-on". I asked Samuel and he answered quickly. "Because it is a silly place to field for a ball."

I saw in his expression the importance of strategy. Our ancestors throughout the war demonstrated the art of strategic planning. This again was another way that he used to demonstrate the ability of our Ashanti ancestors. I remember the story he told us about Sir Alexander Bustamante and how Busta escaped the arrest by the soldiers. Samuel said that there was a large gathering of people at Parade and that the people were there to listen to Busta who was going to talk about how to solve the injustice being done to the working class poor. As Busta came on the scene, the crowd of people cheered and the soldiers were ready with their guns drawn to arrest him. He entered the crowd and as he emerged, the crowd parted to give him way. Busta with his hand in the military salute started to march through the crowd singing the Jamaica National Anthem which then was "God Save Our Gracious Queen." At the sound of the National Anthem, the soldiers rested their guns, joined in the salute to the Crown and Busta marched safely through the crowd. Samuel had a smile on his face at the end of his story. I believe he told this story to demonstrate our capacity to think on our feet and overcome any situation. This was the legacy he had to pass on to us.

Family members who lived in Kingston met on Sunday afternoons at what we called "Kindah." Our meetings were convened at the corner of Smith Lane and Beeston Street. Understand that kindah was more than a physical point of reference like the Kindah tree in Accompong. Kindah was wherever we are because we are family. We believe that where ever Maroons meet in good spirit, the spirit of the African ancestors will gather. These meeting were informative as well as recreational. Samuel and the other men played dominoes or ludo. Interestingly enough the gathering was only for men. The information shared at the meeting was later given to the women at home. Samuel particularly shared the information with my Aunt V.

Elizabeth Salmon nee Rowe Ma Betsy, Aunt Betsy, was the oldest child. She was known as Ma Betsy in Accompong. My sisters and I called her Aunt Betsy. She was born in 1896. My father was the second child. The other siblings who followed Samuel were Uncle Israel or Baba (barber); he was a barber; Aunt V, Vertella Rowe; Estella Mc Kenzie, Sister Mack; Levi Rowe, bullah; Mathias (Selvin) Rowe and Uriah Rowe. Uncle Selvin is alive as I write this book. He lives at Gypsun in Accompong.

5

THE FAMILY CONNECTION

The Ashanti and Coromante and CongonMaroons intermarried over the years. Samuel said that this custom was fostered by Kojo as a means to carry on the population and continue living as they did. Samuel objected to the practice. He comments that he was marrying within the family. I knew that he did because immediately after he told us that the Accompong Maroons were one Royal family. He then said to us, "the name Rowe originated in Accompong Town and was the surname of Kojo." Samuel was direct, informative and humble. He continued. "Wherever you go in Jamaica and you find someone with the surname "Rowe", you are related." Now years later as I check my roots I find that there is either a maternal or a paternal relationship between Maroons from Accompong.

Samuel said it; I believe it and that settled it. Samuel always knew how to connect his informal classroom theory with our practical experiences. It was as if he had set as his lifelong goal a mission to pump every ounce of the aspects of successful living into our lives. So it was not an accident that this information was given to me at the dawn of my womanhood, my first period or menarche. I was eleven years old. Samuel was the first to know that it had happened. He was the first to know of this issue, no pun intended. My body gave me no warning and I was in need of technical support. I was the first of my sisters to reach this milestone. Samuel was at home. My mother was at work. What was I to do? I asked myself. I was not afraid, only unprepared. This event is so private and secret. I know that my mother went through this "thing" because every month lily-white bird's eye napkins waved on our laundry line in the hot noonday sun and no baby was in the home. These napkins must be in hiding somewhere in the house. I dare not search. Maybe I should know. What else could I do?

I remember Samuel and how he carried me in his arms to Ward Theatre. This, however, is a more personal institution and I believe that my mother should have warned me. I had no choice but to tell Samuel. Naturally, he immediately thought of a solution. His first response was towards me. It was a comment. "Why didn't your mother show and tell you what to do"? Without saying another word, Daddy went to a drawer, removed a napkin, showed me how to fold it and put it on then gave me the folded napkin. He rose to the occasion on yet another formative moment in my life.

He said there were twelve Rowe brothers and three sisters. They were the grandsons and granddaughter of Kojo and they were all born in Accompong. James Rowe, Samuel's father, and my grandfather was one of these men. The lesson today from Samuel was to alert me to my ancestral roots and deter any amorous engagement within the tribe. More importantly, he wanted me to know how closely connected we were to Kojo. Today two hundred and seventy one years since the Peace Treaty was signed, the surname Rowe remains the most common name in Accompong and wherever Accompong Maroons are found in the Diaspora. So how did the Rowe name spread outside Accompong? After the war ended and the Peace Treaty was signed between the British and Kojo, my ancestors were free to travel throughout Jamaica. The men traveled outside of Accompong to conduct business. My grandfather made rope. He traveled regularly to the South to sell his product. Nightingale Grove in NewMarket, St. Elizabeth was a place frequented by my grandfather. It was at Nightingale Grove that my grandfather James met my Uncle Selvin's mother. James took her to Accompong and Uncle Selvin was born there.

The brothers and sisters were:

James Rowe, Samuel's father,
Jack Rowe,
Edgar Rowe,
Henry Alfred Rowe,
Charles Rowe,
Esau, Bah Pigeon,
Emmanuel Rowe,
Jeffery Rowe,
Peter Rowe,
Richard Rowe,
Thomas Rowe,
Masa- Bandu.

The names are not in order of birth. These men were the propagators of the "Rowe" lineage. There were sisters as well; however, the female contribution to propagation is silent. Silent because as the women married they discontinued the use of the surname Rowe. For example, my aunt Betsy, Elizabeth Rowe, became Elizabeth Salmon after she married Joseph Salmon. All her children, my cousins, dropped the name Rowe. We know however that we all share the same paternal grandfather, James Rowe, one of the twelve Rowe brothers. Samuel said that Kojo's slave name was Rowe and that the Rowe name is indigenous to Accompong. The slave name Rowe is the most common surname in Accompong. You will find many other surnames in Accompong and in the other Maroon communities outside Accompong.

6

SAMUEL, THE HERBS AND ROOTS MEDECINE MAN

Samuel's father, James Rowe, was also called Doc. Samuel told me that my grandfather James was a bush doctor. He was well versed in the herbs and their many uses. Herbs were used to cure different ailments both external and internal. The high note of my grandfather's career was the healing of a man who reportedly had some type of venereal disease. It was reported to me that the man was referred to my grandfather after traditional treatment regimen failed.

My grandfather, James, was described as an agile man. He would jump from log to log as he gathered several different bushes. James then boiled the bushes and gave the mixture to the man to drink. After a week of this treatment, all the man's symptoms were gone and never returned. There is also the case of the man with the sore on his foot. He, too, came for treatment. I was told that James gathered different herbs, rubbed them together and secured it on the sore with a cloth dressing.

When James removed the dressing several days later, a long needle came from out of the man's foot and the wound healed.

Samuel also knew the use of the herbs. In the early fifties, there was an outbreak of dengue fever in Jamaica. My sister Una and I contracted the illness. We were roasting with fever and rigors, called "ague". As sick as I was, I heard my father discussing with my mother that he would send to Accompong to get some of the "thing". They were very secretive as they deliberated their clandestine operation. How would they get the message to Accompong? Who would bring the "thing"? The train from Kingston to Montego Bay railway was running at that time. In a short time the logistics of the Mission was settled. They would send a message to Accompong via some contact at the Coronation Market and my mother would pick up the package from that contact. They did not have cell phones at that time.

Can you imagine how the early Maroons communicated from Accompong in the North West of the Island to Portland in the East? A formidable task I suppose; but they did. The herb, collie weed (ganja) and the other bushes were sent the following day. The Mission was accomplished. This speedy response is indicative of the Maroon connection and our ability to respond to the need of each other.

The remarkable networking machinery that existed among my forebearers is still present and ever more sophisticated now in the 21st Century. Our link with our fellow Maroons is phenomenal. My ancestors assured a sustainable communication system through their deliberate efforts to promote familial loyalty. I wonder sometime if there is a residual spiritual transference of communicative powers and connectivity between us Maroons.

My father supervised as my mother boiled a few leaves from the collie weed (ganja), gave us some to drink and used some with other bush to give us a traditional medicinal bush steam bath. We sat on a washboard that was placed across a large metal wash pan. Our feet were immersed in the pan of hot boiled bushes leaves including the collie weed. Later I learned that the other bushes were probably, fever grass, pimento bush, ginger root, horse bath, jackeny bush and rosemary. These bushes are the bushes that produce heat and they are used to reduce fever.

They had no Tylenol, Paradmol, Paracetamol nor Cetamol. We were fully draped with a sheet to get the full effect from the steam and the bath. The sheet covered our heads, was draped from our heads over the pan, folded in one area then continued to the floor. My sister and I sat closely on the washboard. We sweated from head to toe and sweated some more. Our bodies shook like thawing jelly in the hands of a person with Parkinson's disease. Our teeth clattered as we inhaled the soothing yet peculiar aroma of the bush bath. Every now and again, our mother would lift the opening in the draped sheet and use the boiled bush to rub over our bodies.

Samuel stayed close and I heard him steadily muttering something, all the time that we were under the sheet. I was really too sick to focus on what he was saying. It was a sound as if he was chanting. What Samuel did outside the steam bath was as important as what happened under the sheet. I am not sure if it was the hot collie weed tea or the steam from the hot bath or his mutterings, but something worked. Shortly after we had the collie weed tea, something happened. My sister and I looked at each other. We did not shake. We felt better. I did not feel like jumping rope but I sure felt better. Samuel's therapeutic regimen worked. The following day we were totally recovered from all signs of the Dengue fever. No fever, no chills, no nothing. Samuel tapped into the ancestral herbal pharmacopoeia and bingo; his knowledge and proper use of the herbs cured us almost instantly.

We weren't sure how we were going to explain this covert mission to our neighbours. We lived in a tenement so privacy was not a frill. Naturally, the next day our neighbours were amazed at our speedy recovery. Everybody was meddling in Samuel's and Irene's business. They were eager to know the cure especially since many other children were ill and some were dying from the disease. They wanted to know what Mr. Rowe used to cure us. Samuel demonstrated again, what he learned from his ancestors; it was a pledge to keep secret what must remain a secret. He taught me how to keep a secret. He taught us not to meddle in other people's business. Leave people's business alone. My parents never revealed the secret to their neighbours. You see, the use of collie weed was illegal. I recall by my father's account that collie weed was first identified in the Cockpit Country. This "wonder weed" was a cure all for many ills. I was told that some of the best collie weed is grown in Accompong in the Cockpit Mountains.

My ancestors were resourceful so they soon identified the many uses for the herb. Word about this "wonder herb" spread about Jamaica like wild fire. Shortly after its discovery in Accompong, collie weed was found in other areas of Jamaica. The older people used the collie weed to boil tea. They never smoked the herb. This tradition of the use of herbal medicine was practiced by my African ancestors and was passed on from one generation to the other.

I am not sure what or who came first to the Cockpit Mountains. I do know however, that at some point in time both the plants and my African ancestors inhabited the same space. Man and environment were engaged in an interaction where each harmoniously cared for each other. With the absence of a pharmaceutical building, lack of a Research and Development budget and research subjects, my ancestors found the herbs and used them. They practiced medicine very much like some of the eastern people, naturally, holistically and skillfully. Many herbs can be found in the Cockpit Mountains. In Accompong, we still have a plethora of medicinal herbs and people who know how to use them.

7

THE CALL TO WAR

The war between the Jamaican Maroons and the British Government ended in 1738. The Abeng was blown to send the message across the Island to the other Maroon communities. It was not a truce. The end of the war was real; a battle that started since 1655 was now ended. This momentous event for my ancestors happened at a place we come to know as Peace Cave. Peace Cave is located in the Cockpit Mountains of The Trelawney Town Maroon of the Sovereign State of Accompong, Jamaica. King George II was the ruling monarch at the time of this history-making event. Two treaties were signed; that is the Leeward Treaty on March 1, 1738 and the Windward Treaty some months later in 1739. This was the end of humans being chased, being hounded like criminals by dogs and being shot at. The attempt to capture and enslave a group of Africans in Jamaica ended. This act to sign a Treaty, daddy said, was the highlight in the history of our African ancestors and the reward for our African ancestors. He said that the British begged for mercy. "The white man went down on his knees and begged Kojo," he laughed. The same time Kojo and his men circle him with guns and swords." Samuel was clear about his report of that day.

He knew that our African ancestors were special and wanted to be sure that we remembered this formidable accomplishment. He wanted the story to be so ingrained in our psyche that nothing in life could erase the great lessons transferred to us by this war. Samuel's stories centered around the fact that our African ancestors were the first Africans in the Western Hemisphere to be freed from slavery, and the determination they developed to do this. The Treaty between our African ancestors and the British in 1738-1739 marked the culmination of the first war that the British lost. The Africans from Ghana defeated the British militia. I often wonder why this significant event is among the missing in the archives of history. Samuel did everything humanly possible to transfer to his daughters the worth and weight of this event in the shaping of our lives and character. He constantly chiseled in our minds the positive beings we are. His every stroke of his hammer against his chisel that cored our minds was done to remove words from our mind such as traitors, pilferers, deserters, to name a few.

Samuel said the Africans had been living peacefully in their different communities in the mountains. The British, he said, launched the attack against the Africans. I wonder at what point did the dynamics of power changed these Ashanti Africans from being "escaped slaves" to becoming the enemies of their British captors. He said the British had successfully beaten the Spanish colonists and now was the time for them to capture the "rebellious, deranged" Ashanti Africans. After all, to them these Africans were the chattel; the price for each was paid. They should not have had the audacity to believe that the privilege of freedom would be placed in their laps; and that the shackles and vestiges of servitude would disintegrate.

I believe that the Africans expected the British to attack them at any time and therefore lived in the anticipation of that day. If they were forcefully removed from their homeland in Africa and purchased for a price, what was there to spare them from being captured again? I believe they lived every day in anticipation of their capture or recapture. Samuel said the Spanish slave owners "let go" the Africans and expected them to assist the Spaniards in their battle against the British. Samuel tells this story with some expression of pity for the Spanish slave owners. "Fools," he would say. "They were foolish. You can't set your enemy free and then expect him to come to your rescue." Why were my African ancestors released and then asked to assist in a battle that was not theirs? As far as Samuel was concerned the Maroons were free and prepared to stay free at all cost. When they chose to stay in the Cockpit Mountains, they made this decision as part of their strategy for success. I believe the plan was to remain in the mountains and wait for the attack from anyone at anytime and in any direction.

Finally when the Spaniards released these Africans, they immediately went to the mountains. A plan for freedom had to be in their minds from the moment of their capture as slaves. They knew that they had to fight to be free. I can hardly think that they were so naïve as to dream that life would be peaceful forever once they escaped to the mountains. After all, they seized an opportunity for freedom and removed themselves from servitude. This action placed them in a precarious position similar to that of illegal aliens. It is only fitting then to think that they would contemplate how and when this state of nirvana would end. When will the British hunters call the hunt? Who started this war and what was at stake?

Samuel's account of the war as told to me was that the British started it and were determined to capture and or kill our ancestors who dared to believe that they were free. Some of my ancestors, who embraced their status of freedom, were now living in the Cockpit Mountains in Trelawney, the mountains of Portland and other areas of St. Catherine and St.Mary. Samuel said the Africans "were living all over Jamaica." Some, the Maroons, he said escaped to the mountainous areas of Jamaica and were living in these mountains long before the sound of war against them was heralded by the British. "They fight with them for over eighty years." Samuel said, "even if the war lasted for one hundred years the British could not win this war." He was positive about this.

The successful outcome of the war for the Maroons shows the intense strategic planning and organization that was operational during the eighty-three years of war, 1655 - 1738-39. All components of battle were planned and organized including the means of communication and style of combat. Theirs was a lateral organizational structure with clearly defined leadership roles. The goal of the organization was "freedom at all cost." Yes, and the members of the organization, were at all times willing to take on any job, assigned or not, as long as the job was a benefit to the accomplishment of the goal—freedom. My ancestors did not stop to negotiate a salary nor embrace an attitude of entitlement. Samuel said that the advantage of freedom was priceless to them . Their agenda was to win the war. Win they must at all cost, a cost not to be borne by them but by the opponents. I say opponents because at times there were internal opponents. These were other Africans. Samuel called them "traitors".

8

THE MEETING PLACE, THE HOUSE
OF PARLIAMENT

Samuel's account about the Maroon warriors was that they would meet at the place called Kindah. The meetings were held as often as was necessary. Samuel said, "they would meet when Kojo call for a meeting." The word Kindah is an African word that means, "We are family." This African word from our ancestors holds true to this very day. Whatever the consequence, we are family; we will act as family and we will conduct ourselves as a family. The code is let no stranger interfere. The mango tree that marks the spot at Kindah is now over two hundred and seventy years old. This historic meeting place is still here in Accompong. Kindah is an area that is special to us Maroons. Once a year on January 6 only, a special celebration feast is held at Kindah in honour of Kojo's birthday and the signing of the Peace Treaty.

The mango tree is now a huge tree and the strength of its many years, the roots, spread out in all directions from the trunk. There are rocks arranged around the trunk and they represent what seems to me to be the seating arrangement for the people who attended the meetings. It is now over three hundred years later and the seats, these rocks, are still prominently embedded into the ground. The roots of this huge tree are solid and spread out as claws between the stone benches. The roots now compete for primary position; however, there is a big stone that commands territorial rights. This stone is placed to suggest that it is the head seat, the place assigned for the leader. The centripetal arrangement of the other seats is so designed to bring the audience as close as possible to the leader or person conducting the meeting. There is little space between each stone.

I started to contemplate how many soldiers were seated and how many were standing during these meetings. Samuel said, "Only a handful of African soldiers were fighting." The seats at Kindah seem to support that the number in the African army was small.

I experience peace as I sit under the mango tree at the place known as Kindah. I feel the connection of spirits of my ancestors and a feeling of power as I sit under the tree and think about those meetings. The movement seems as alive to me now as it did over two hundred years ago. I sit on a stone that is the biggest of all the stones. I believe it was Kojo's seat. It is the head stone. As I inspect the meeting place and the seating arrangement at Kindah, I recognize that the selection of this site was also well thought out by my ancestors.

When I am at Kindah, I realize that the location is also the best lookout site in Accompong. The land around the tree is flat. The foliage in the surrounding area and location of this meeting place afforded the security and privacy for discussion of sensitive strategic plans. Samuel said it was at Kindah that the African leaders would gather to discuss recent events of the war. In present day vernacular, they would "conduct debriefing sessions" and plan their next military maneuver. The place Kindah was the "Pentagon" or "Military Head Quarters"

Samuel said, "The British called our people runaway because the word 'runaway' made us look like we are savages." He was annoyed with the British for conferring such a label. He knew better. I believe that the title of a savage also would dictate the manner in which the combat maneuvers would be justified by the British terrorists. However, savages or not, the African soldiers had to prepare themselves for battle. Consider "runaways" meeting to initiate military strategy for-on-the-ground combat. A strategy would embrace and activate all of their skills, tenacity, bravery and intelligence.

Travel this mental journey with me for a moment and concentrate on some Ashanti Africans removed from their homes in Africa. They meet in Jamaica to plan and chart their course for a successful war strategy. They had no survival manual; or on the other hand, did they? I believe that prudence would dictate that such a tool would not be efficient in the execution of a strategic recall. Their combat had them on the run most times. These soldiers undoubtedly must depend on their memory as they planned for their tactical operations. What brilliant minds the Maroons had. What a capacity for memory and instant recall. I find it overwhelming and difficult to articulate the essence of this fact; their tenacity, bravery and skill.

The meeting habitat afforded them with little else than rocks as seats. The absence of a computer, telephone, a filing cabinet, a fax machine, desks and writing paper did nothing to alter their plan to win the war. The gap between now and then is relative. The missing technological links were not seen as obstacles but rather they forged their course in spite of what today seems like obstacles. Imagine a meeting of the minds and the spirits as they planned for success. The Spirits had to connect. Like Moses, they used what they had.

After the meeting at Kindah, someone would blow the abeng to pass
on what had happened and relate plans for the battle. They also would
beat the drums to sound out the message. Kojo would stay in
Accompong and the surrounding areas while Nanny went off to
Portland or one of the other Maroon communities. Kojo and Nanny
were the Commanders in Chief. Nanny directed the African soldiers in
the Windward areas and Kojo directed the African soldiers in the
Leeward areas. Both planned the war. Both fought in the war on
all fronts. According to Samuel, Nanny was Kojo's confidant and
biological sister.

The stories related by Samuel portray Kojo and Nanny as
inseparable. Their sincere love, respect and commitment to each were
essential to their success. History has remained silent on this matter and
Kojo is obliterated from accounts of the war. Whatever the reason for
this external silence or omission of the bond between Nanny and Kojo,
I know that Samuel was certain of his account. The descendants in
Accompong continue to this day to speak of both Kojo and Nanny.

9

COCKPIT COUNTRY

The leaders of the Organization, Nanny and Kojo, employed a strategy that incorporated the entire expanse of the mountainous Cockpit terrain. They clearly understood and applied the instruction given to Moses, "use what is in your hand." They had in their hands all the tools to win the war and win it they did. Samuel said that, "The cockpit was the best battleground that the African soldiers had. They moved from place to place all over the mountain range." He said, "Kojo and his people knew the mountains like the back of their hand." Their strategy of defense would be to use the natural and intricate design of the total terrain they had to defend. The Cockpit Country is mountainous with heavy forest and vegetation. The mountains cascade to the low-lying areas that are also forested. Samuel said, "They had them all over the cockpit."

When Samuel first told me about the cockpit, I thought it was a mysterious place and that somehow hidden in the mountains were the answers to win the war. I have since discovered that the mountain and surrounding areas were indeed ideal for the type of combat they had to fight. In the Mountains, the African soldiers had home court advantage. They moved from place to place within the Cockpit Country as the British soldiers savagely attacked. The British were no match for the Cockpit Mountains or for the Ashanti warriors.

Take a visit to the Cockpit country and you will understand this phenomenon as you experience the natural terrain of the Cockpit. It is only then that you will appreciate why my African ancestors at all times had the advantage of "home court". Samuel said, "There was absolutely no way that the British soldiers would win the war as long as the African fighters remained in the Cockpit Mountains." The many caves, springs, rivers sink holes and almost perilous trails required intricate knowledge and skills to conquer this magnificent terrain. Samuel consistently emphasized this point to us. The seasonal rainfall also made the terrain slippery and the clay soil added to the challenge of navigation in the woods.

10

THE AFRICAN SOLDIERS

In those days, women were not relegated to a domestic platform. There was no need to establish a feminist movement. Theirs was a role of inclusion. Win the war we must. Remember, "We are family." Their strategy of gender inclusion was one that eliminated the chance of the slightest distraction of a mistaken identity of a role. Any form of distraction was seen as a shift from reaching the goal. Such a shift was immediate cause for concern and retooling. Except for Nanny, Samuel said, "very few women were actually fighting." The women were few in numbers and were not engaged in combat. They were the support team in this fragile combat environment; fragile because the combat zone had many other inhabitants and a dynamic characteristics. The women saw to it that when the men returned from combat that they cared for them. Kojo was responsible for making sure that all members of the community understood and embraced their role in the struggle.

A leader was in the making at all times, be it a male or a female. They were prepared to fight to retain their freedom and would do so as long as it would take. A leader must be in preparation at all times. The expectations and directions were simple and clear. How then will the African communicate the passing of the baton in this fragile environment? This is something that was taken for granted. After all what did my ancestors know about communicating? Samuel said they knew a lot. Let us listen to them for a moment.

11

STRATEGIC COMMUNICATION

According to Samuel, the lines of communication between our African soldiers were clear with the Abeng. Without the existence of cell phones, satellite antennas, cable lines or internet access, the Maroons used a cow's horn (the Abeng) to communicate throughout the Island. The sound of the Abeng is audible for nine miles or fifteen Kilometers.

How is this priceless communication tool engineered? The cow's horn is the hard outer layer or keratin from the horn. The core of the horn consists of bone, which is covered by a porous mineral matter, blood vessels, marrow and other living matter. The sheath of the bone consists of keratin, a hard substance. A thin layer of tissue lies between the bone and the keratin sheath. When the animal dies the tissue rots and makes it easy for the keratin sheath to be removed from the bone. (www.Cowboy Way.com) This keratin sheath forms the instrument the Maroons call the Abeng. The horn lasts a lifetime. The original Abeng is in safekeeping at an undisclosed location.   The Abeng has three openings. The smallest opening is placed at the mouth almost as if one is blowing a horn. About an inch from the smallest opening is another opening that is used by the blower to control the sound as it is blown through the widest opening of the horn. The blower uses a finger to control and alter the sound.

Samuel said our African soldiers developed the skill and art of blowing the Abeng to the extent that they altered the sounds to create different meanings with each sound. I remember the first time that I heard the sound of the Abeng. It was a peculiar distinct sound and the echo hung in the air as if waiting for the next note. Some sounds were short and some were long. It had no rhythm; I cannot put a dance step to match the sound. It is a sound similar to the howling of a dog without that crescendo and rhythm. It is a sound that demands you listen; sometimes it was an eerie sound. As the message went forth through the airwaves, the sound would be picked up and transmitted to the next Abeng blower until the message reached its final destination.

Remember my ancestors were stripped of everything including their dignity during their passage from Africa to Jamaica. I believe this means of communicating so effectively may have been crafted, studied and mastered here in the Cockpit Mountains and transferred to other Maroon communities across Jamaica. I make this assumption since Samuel said the attack started against the Maroons in the Trelawny area of the Cockpit and later spread to the eastern part of the island. Samuel said that the battle was all over the cockpit.

The Abeng is still blown today in Accompong and other Maroon communities across Jamaica. The sound of this instrument now signals an important event; meetings, the annual January 6th Celabration of Kojo's birthday, to announce the death of a Maroon, at digging of the grave and at funeral services. The mountain formation and the lack of competing noise makes it easy for the sound from the Abeng to travel almost unhindered. If you shout, you can hear the echo of your voice as it reverberates across the mountainside. I find it awesome each time I experience this in the mountains, whether it is in Accompong or other areas of the Cockpit. I hear the sound of frogs; we call them "bull frogs". I am not sure why. I hear the frogs croak, the lizards just show up and you sense the presence of a tiny creature. I listen to the cricket and its chirping sound, the woodpecker sounding like an out of tune base guitar being played by a frantic person, the bat as it soars through the night flapping its wings, the humming bird flipping its wings faster that the propeller of an helicopter, the whispering of the banana leaves, the sound of the banana fruit as it sends out each hand of banana, the ewe goat as she calls for the ram; the hog grunting for the next spot of mud, the crowing cock at the wake of dawn and now these days sometimes during the day, the water as it spews from the spring or rushes down the mountain. I hear many sounds.

My ancestors likewise must have heard many sounds. They must have had a keen ear for all kinds of sound in order to master the ability to send, receive and act on classified messages. Can you imagine the responsibility and sharpness of our African ancestors? Samuel would relate this tale with such engaging attitude that it was hard for me not to absorb the significance and stealth of this major achievement. Every time he would tell the story about the Africans and their use of the Abeng to communicate with one another, without hesitation, he would quickly add, "And the British soldiers had to ride horses to take their messages from place to place." This would be followed with a smile readable only by the twinkle in his eyes; the curve from the lines on either side of his mouth; the faint quiver of his lips and the erect posture of his torso. Yes! Samuel knew how to say much with few words by his expressions and body language. I learned well how to interpret his non-verbal cues.

If the British had to carry their messages by way of the horse express, naturally you can understand their dilemma. I need not insult your intelligence to report on the outcome of this method compared to the use of the Abeng. My father Samuel said no more to me. I am sure you can figure out what happened. My ancestors must have mastered sound and language and combined these elements to produce a sensitive and strategic form of communication. This was the language that the Africans used to outsmart the British soldiers. Consider for a while that our African warriors came with their different African language. They must have heard other languages during their passage from Africa to Jamaica. On arrival in Jamaica, the Spanish spoke yet another language and later came the British with English.

My African ancestors were linguists. They combined their African vernacular, Spanish and English languages to produce a new Creole language. Samuel said it was a language that "confused the British". I believe that they mastered the skill of internal strategic communication as they prepared for the day of impending attacks and the mastery of external communication was perfected during combat. I make this assumption because he said the African soldiers said very little during combat. They were action oriented. Kill the enemy. The opponents, the British, were counter-attacked by people who said little, moved like ghosts, sometimes looked like trees and were unbeatable.

Samuel had an enviable ability to engage us in any aspect of our ancestors and their fight. He would lift his chest, throw back his shoulders, give his upper torso a slight but noticeable shake and project a strong commanding posture as he spoke. He had an attitude much like the teens do today except his shake was subtle. His shake missed the side-to-side and forward backward gyrations of the head and neck. His attitude was neither arrogance nor defiance; it was a posture of pride. It was a pride that was marinated in the spirit of humility and served with grace and love. I have seen Samuel in this stance so many times before. This time, the topic was the events of the war. He took me into the imaginary world of the combat zone. I listened to the Abeng. I heard the messages. I spend little time with my fellow African soldiers as we decide in unison the next move.

He said that the fighting was constant. I cannot imagine that fighting took place only at daytime. The British would send troops from England as soon as the African fighters destroyed the ones that were here. They had to move to counter attack. In spite of ideological differences, the ancestors recognized the value and benefit of a united force. They knew unequivocally that their common good would only be achieved through the unity of the fighters. Unity had to be first. These Africans considered themselves as soldiers all fighting for the same cause. The successful mobilization of their other African brothers and sisters across Jamaica speaks to their intellectual genius.

The Ashanti Africans were under attack across Jamaica. The enemy was advancing from all sides. The British attacks were launched on all fronts. War was declared. Evidently, the attack was imminent. As far as the British were concerned, these Africans were presumptuous to entertain the notion of resistance and freedom with the resultant privileges. As if the horrendous passage from Africa to Jamaica was not enough, my ancestors were now forced to fight the enemy to keep this freedom which they won when the Spanish fled the island leaving them free. What would be the consequences if my ancestors lost the battle? Samuel was emphatic! A loss to the enemy was not an option for the Ashanti. "We must win."

Surely as the British must have deferred their plan to attack, the Ashanti soldiers likewise planned for a counter attack. Naturally, the

Africans objective was to stay free at all cost. This objective was echoed by all Africans across the Ashanti and other African communities on the island. The movement of resistance to being enslaved had to be embraced by all the Africans. A sense of togetherness had to permeate throughout the African camp. It seems to me that this position of unity was not an option for them but a prerequisite to their success. They must have had a fundamental principle that said first let us commit to agree that we are free then set out on a mission never to be enslaved no matter what the consequences. A consensus about their freedom must have been burned into their psyche thereby eliminating the entrance of any other idea. The war was on. The war was real. It was the British against the Africans.

The Ashanti soldiers were organized. I have no clue as to the name of any drill sergeant. As far as Samuel reported, Kojo was the person who guided the soldiers into strategy. I know however, that Kojo must have been the drill sergeant. I can only imagine that their success was due to someone's ability to train. It is the drill sergeant's responsibility to train, engage and deliver a good soldier. There was no draft pick; no application pool to select from or recruit. Samuel said that from time to time, other African slaves would join the ranks but the process of selection was stringent. Theirs was a lateral organizational structure rich with natural human resources. The code of ethics was precise and stringent. Kojo and Nanny ruled with power, clarity and their belief in God.

12

MILITARY GARMENT

All were attired in the same military fatigue. The garment was made from the bark of trees such as mahoe, jimmie and trumpet and from clothing left from their Spanish slave occupation. Most often little or no clothing was worn on the torso. The military fatigue was a real one. It was as real as the foliage that they used to drape themselves from head to toe. Their uniform was practical, easily accessible and sustainable. I assume that much thought went into the care and maintenance of the military garment worn by the African soldiers. Clothing was appropriate for the tropical climate and allowed for ease in movement among the vegetation. Samuel said that the African soldiers used herbs as part of their camouflage. He said the ancestors rubbed the herbs all over their bodies and as a result, the dogs could not find them as they traversed the mountainous terrain. Think about it. The absence of clothing was also a strategy in their plan to be successful. The ability of the Africans to think of the best method to outfit them in combat is commendable.

My father said the British soldiers were dressed in heavy red woolen coats, pants, boots and hats. They carried a bayonet, a rifle and a sword. The clothing was a hindrance to the mission. Consider the British soldier trying to navigate through the sometimes-dense foliage and the difficulty they must experience as they secure their weapons during flight. Their military fatigue was not adapted to the Jamaican climate or terrain.

13

MESS HALL

Sustainable utensils were manufactured from calabash (packy), wood and bamboo. The husk of the calabash was used as a dish or a cup and they carved spoons from wood. Meals were made from the meat of hogs, baldpate birds, pigeon, barble dove, a yam called himber and sometimes a vegetable called jocotu. Hogs could be found all over the Cockpit. Samuel said that our ancestors were classified as wild because they hunted hogs for food. He would say to us, "There is no tame hog. All hogs are wild." Mess hall was anywhere suitable for the cooking and preparing of meals. It was anywhere a fire could be made without bringing attention to them.

The mess hall was as transitory as the combat area. I believe that they learned to live with nature therefore food was not always cooked. Did they sometimes harvest honey from hives in the caves? How did they survive? The art to sustain and nurture themselves within the confines of the land of wood and water tells me that some research was ongoing at all times.

14

INSURGENTS

Samuel told me that there were Ashanti traitors among the Africans. Dissidents were a distraction to the objective and therefore had to be eradicated at all cost. "Kojo would "chop off their heads" my father said bluntly. "Yes, Kojo would dispose of them expeditiously by cutting off their heads" he repeated. His face was pensive and hollow. I did not ask for an explanation. I know that I was old enough to understand someone's head being removed from his body. A court martial was not possible, practical or available. That system of punishment did not exist among them. Kojo the leader and Commander in Chief was a man with zero tolerance for deception of any sort. Nothing would interfere with their objective to stay free. When my father first told me of the fate of these subversive Africans, it was difficult for me to understand Kojos' method of disposition of the "rebellious" African. I now understand that in combat there are times when the soldier must act quickly to survive. A traitor is a traitor and therefore a hindrance to the mission to stay free. Combat was the way that the African soldiers would achieve the goal of freedom. If you break the secret bond of the mission, you weaken the strength of the collective efforts. The leaders did not tolerate deception or anything that threatened their community and their freedom.

15

AFRICAN TROOPS

Yes, during the eighty-three years of war, the Commander-in-Chief of the Maroons had no troops waiting to be drafted into service; neither was there a recruiting post. Samuel named other troop members. They were brothers and a sister of Kojo. They were Accompong, Quashi, Cuffie, Quao, Johnnie and Ninna. I believe others were involved in the war; however, it was Kojo and Nanny who led the Africans to the end. Samuel talked much about Kojo and Nanny and wanted us to learn from these two great leaders.

Were the Ashanti Africans, soldiers? Certainly, they were soldiers par excellence. Only a trained soldier can engage in combat with an opponent who is fully equipped, and yet, suffer little or no casualty. These Ashanti soldiers were not guerillas. They were peacemakers. They were kind, loving and giving. Samuel used this jingle to remind us of the exponential benefits of being kind, loving and giving.

Do all the good you can.

In all the ways, you can.

For all the people you can.

Just as long as you can.

Samuel would then tells us the story of this man who tried to impart this lesson of kindness to his son. The poor boy would say:

Do all the good you scan

In all the ways you scan

For all the people you scan

Just as long as you scan.

The man would beat the boy because the lad was not getting the word "can" correctly. Each time the boy's father said, "can" the lad said "scan".

Samuel smiled and in sympathy, he shook his head from left to right. "The boy repeated the song a few times. He tried to say each word just as his father did but he could not." In utter frustration, the father gave up. Samuel then calmly explained, "The boy had a lisp." As we say today, "he was physically challenged" and therefore had difficulty when he tried to pronounce the word "can".

Samuel wanted to show us how we waste our God given potential when we labour on the unimportant. This was an opportunity for the boy's father to teach love to the boy; instead, it became what seems to be a senseless act of reprimand. What a loss. This behavior was typical of the British soldiers. Their intent was to destroy my African ancestors. They did not come for their good or to do well by them. The British soldiers spent over eighty years trying to do evil while my ancestors were dancing around them and killing them in their advance.

My ancestors were brave, fearless men and women who received their military training from their military leaders, Nanny and Kojo. Some of the training I believe had to be on the job training as actual battles were taking place at all times. A training camp was not practical because such a place would provide limitations in the strategic use of the landscape. Samuel said that the army in Accompong consisted of a "hand full of people mostly men", relative to the numbers available to the British. This information was military secret and highly classified. The British soldiers were not privy to this information. This fact confounded the British soldiers as they engineered attack after attack on the Africans and yet victory for them was not in sight.

Samuel said the Africans fooled the British soldiers into believing that they were large in numbers. I watched Samuel as he again shook his head slowly from side to side. His eyes were partially closed as if to reduce the glare into them. He was deep in thought. I had seen that posture of his many times. He did not entertain dialogue at this point in the conversation. He was at a crossroad of fate and wonder. His was not a lonely journey. Each moment pulled him closer to the strength, spirituality and reality of our Maroon ancestors. I will never ever forget this experience.

I have witnessed my father in this pensive mood. I was sucked into his experience by his depth and spiritual pull. The look of disbelief on his face was painful yet sympathetic. His eyes grew smaller as he pondered the shallow thinking of the British soldiers. I believe that he really wanted to understand what appeared to be the simple mind of the British soldiers. They were after the Africans like hunters and the Africans always escaped; they were slippery and skillful. You would not find the African soldiers at the same venue twice. They mastered the art of movement of the troops. This feat was a successful one because the soldiers combined their collective knowledge of their environment to map out the terrain.

When Samuel tells the story, I am reminded of the story of the Scarlet Pimpernel. "They seek him here they seek him there, they seek him everywhere; the damned elusive Pimpernel." The Maroon soldiers were branded as wild people, but they were skilled, elusive. They operated with the element of surprise and controlled their military maneuvers.

The Africans in preparation for the day of combat had mapped the Cockpit Country, studied the mountains and therefore had full command of the terrain. Samuel said my ancestors studied "every nook and cranny of the Cockpit." They knew where every cave, sinkhole and areas of quick sand was located. They truly lived in harmony with the environment; each one was a successful practicing environmentalist.

They studied in detail the topography of the Mountains and mastered the art of navigating these elaborate masterpieces of God's creation. Since the Maroons had limited manpower, the Mountains provided them with the escape from attack. They engineered footpaths that connected Nanny Town in the center, to Flagstaff in the North West, Elderslie, and Cooks Bottom in the mid west, Aberdeen, Quick Step, Trelawney and Content in the North, Fullers Wood in the South, Wait-a-bit and Portland in the East. These are a few of the Maroon villages Samuel talked about. He said Accompong was first called Nanny Town. Kojo named the Town "Accompong" in honor of his brother Accompong.

16

THE COMMANDER IN CHIEF, NANNY

Nanny was known for her spiritual powers and ability to use her spiritual gifts. She was not working obeah. Samuel told us about Nanny and her spiritual achievements. His report was that Nanny was responsible for the deaths of many British soldiers during the war. She exercised her spiritual gift to do many great things. Samuel said she walked in the faith and belief of a sovereign powerful God. He said, "She never fears anyone." Famous among her exploits was her ability to single-handedly annihilate a troop of soldiers. Although killing another person is not a commendable act, Nanny killed the soldiers because they were fighting a war and she had to kill the enemy or be killed.

I believe that the Maroon soldiers depended on her skills, spirituality and stealth. Samuel told us that Nanny traveled alone most times. She was an army of one. Albeit surrounded by many spiritual soldiers. Samuel told us that the British soldiers fired at the Africans and

Nanny would stand in front of them and catch the bullets with her behind. When my sister and I first heard this story, we were in shock.

"Explain what you mean by that Daddy." Samuel did not oblige. I spent days caught up in the aura of such an achievement and ruminated on the process.

My sisters and I were flabbergasted. We spent a long time deliberating the anatomical feasibility of such a thing. Did Nanny have a big behind? Was she graciously endowed in her posterior? Was she wearing a pad around her hip? Moreover, if she was, somebody should tell the story about extracting the shells from such a pad. Somehow, our young minds would not allow our thoughts to progress beyond the human anatomy of Nanny's buttocks. We wondered what it was about Nanny that sheltered her from these bullets.

My sisters and I had exhausted our reasoning abilities and our father was not ready to explain. We tried to catch him off guard by asking him to tell us stories. He had a favourite jingle that he loved and it goes like this:

"He sells sea shells on the sea shore and all the shells that he sells are sea shells from the sea shore."

The catch is to say the jingle as fast as you possibly can. This exercise requires deep concentration and your ability to stay the course to the finish line. We knew that he loved this jingle so we craftily engaged him in the exercise to say the jingle. The objective to say the jingle is to repeat the words as fast as possible without a mistake. If you made a mistake, you had to start over from the beginning. Our collective effort was to melt his power of concentration and wait for him to be caught off-guard. How clever! We thought.

Samuel never flinched, never faltered. We realized that this man was grounded and unmovable. We had another jingle! Ah! Maybe we could get him with that one. "Peter Piper picked a pickle. If Peter Piper picked the pickle...." That did not work either. He was having fun as we engaged in this mind exercise. Samuel had the upper hand. He wanted us to strengthen our power to concentrate.

What must be done for him to tell us more and answer our question? Why was Nanny able to withstand and not succumb to these deadly attacks? We asked Samuel repeatedly to explain this mystery, but he kept silent on the matter. Each time we asked for an explanation we had to be satisfied with his of his telling of the incident.

He told the story repeatedly. He was not ready to say more to us. Then one day I said to him, "Daddy, I can't understand how Nanny caught the bullets with her bottom and she didn't die. How come her bottom was not blown away?" Where did the bullets go"?

I was somehow expecting the same repetition and account of the story all over again. However, this time Samuel replied. "The same way she had a big pot boiling with no fire under the pot and she is stirring the pot but nothing is in the pot. In addition, the British soldiers see her and cannot touch her. Instead, as they looked at Nanny stirring the pot, man, they dropped dead in front of her." Wow! Did we really have an answer? Now I was confused.

Samuel stopped there. From his facial expression you could tell he had said something that he felt I ought to understand. This was not the answer for my satisfaction. "How is this possible?" I asked him repeatedly and again. After a while, my sisters stopped the queries. I wanted a plausible answer to satisfy my sense of reasoning. The whole episode seemed more than real to me. I wanted an answer that was real to me. I wanted a real tangible meaning to this seemingly bizarre story.

It was just like the many times that my father tried to teach me conversational Spanish. I wanted to see the written Spanish language to understand the spoken language. I know that I must see clearly to understand. Didactic must be followed with the practical. How else will I pass this information to my children? How will I share this anomaly with anyone? A rump catching bullets and a pot boiling with nothing in the pot and no fire under the pot; yeah! Right. His response did not add up. I have come to realize that this ability to translate different languages must be a skill of my ancestors. He knew I wanted to get an answer that made sense to me. My father had a keen sense of interpreting a person's mood and expression. I knew that from day to day he was sizing me up to see if I had given up on his answer.

Without prompting from my sister or myself, he started another story about Nanny. I remember the day clearly. I was at the dining table doing my homework. Samuel said, "People believe that Nanny was a heavy science worker because some of the Maroons worked science. Nanny was a very spiritual woman."

"What is science Daddy?"

"Science is obeah." I accepted his answer and never raised the subject again. I knew then that obeah is "bad".

What then is the super spiritual connection that allows Nanny to catch bullets with her buttocks and kill soldiers who dared to look in her empty pot that boiled with no fire under it?

Bingo! I found the connection. Right there in the Book of First Kings Chapter 18: 22-39. It is the story of the prophet Elijah and Ahab. Indulge yourself in the reading of this story in the Bible and use it to grasp the significance of the use of spiritual powers in the Maroon wars.

Africans know and believe in the omnipotent power of God that is available to all who believe in this power. Successful use of the power however is dependent on being in right standing with God Almighty. My African ancestors were strong believers in God Almighty. I believe they studied the word of God and knew the Word of God and practiced living the Word before they were stolen from their homeland. Their deep-rooted spirituality was crucial in the development of their survival and winning strategies. They knew how to trust in God, how to call on God and that God is real. This reality they experience daily through contact with everything in the world around them. Nanny was not proving anything to the British soldiers; she was demonstrating the power of her God.

Given the steadfast and relentless attack by the British soldiers, our African soldiers had to pull all stops to win. They understood the power of the Spirit of God and were not afraid to use it. Needless to say, the British soldiers were confounded. Nanny was the person identified as the Spiritual Leader. This state secret was well guarded by the Maroons. Samuel said that there was another woman named Nina. She was also a female Maroon soldier. He said Nina was just as spiritually connected as Nanny was; however, he said it was Nanny who took control and exercised her responsibilities as a soldier and leader.

17

WEAPONS

Samuel said that the African soldiers amassed an arsenal of swords, rifles and bayonets from the British soldiers they killed. He said the Africans did not have the luxury of their own arsenal. They would fix the weapons for use. I believe they spent time to learn how to care for the weapons that they captured from the British. My assumption is that my ancestors studied and mastered the skill in the repair and maintenance of the swords, rifles and bayonets. Samuel also said that the Africans made spears and knives from wood. He said that they used stones to sharpen the wood. Imagine that my ancestors used the crudest of equipment to keep their artillery and ammunition in good working condition at all times. This achievement is noteworthy and speaks to the level of intelligence of our ancestors. They knew how to use their brains. Think of how they mastered these skills. Maybe they had a person whose responsibility was to service the weapon and then share this skill with the other African soldiers. I believe that even in this area of securing weapons, my ancestors excelled because they embraced the strength of unity. I believe that at the point of combat anything lethal was considered a weapon at the time of attack. The vine of the sancoma tree was probably used to strangle the opponent. Samuel said that they would "break the neck" of the British soldiers. They must have used anything they had.

18

THE TREATY AND PEACE CAVE

What led to the British calling for an end to the war and the Peace Treaty that terminated it? Samuel said, "Kojo and his men were at Old Town waiting for the British to attack. So they came so we killed them. We knew how many British soldiers there were."

I asked daddy, "How they knew and the British did not kill them?" Old Town was flat land and therefore the battlefield was open except for areas where the foliage cascade to form a natural cover. According to my father Old Town was the place where my Maroon ancestors lured the British and kept them in battle until they surrendered. He said, "Kojo and his men used the leaves to wrap up themselves. They wrapped from head to toe and only left a little part to see. In addition, they would stand still like a tree. Boy as soon as a soldier passes one of Kojo's men they would kill him." Samuel's lips parted not in a smile, but in a questioning grimace. He continued. "Kojo and the men kept on beating the British."

Many British soldiers lost their lives during this period of defense. Gravesites of the British soldiers are still visible at Old Town and represent some of the British Casualties. Their loss was unbearable for them. My father said that when the British realized that their most recent replenishment of soldiers were all dead the British went to Old Town to ask Kojo to stop the fighting. I believe that they must have called out for mercy and as Samuel said, "Begged" for the fighting to stop. I can only picture such a scenario given the fact that the strategic planning of my ancestors was unbeatable.

The war was now over eighty years. Samuel said the war was continuous. For years the British were out-smarted, out-performed and killed by the Maroons. Somewhere, somehow, the British Commander-in-Chief had to make a decision to end the war. Which of us under normal circumstances could withstand such a prolonged beating? Remember, our ancestors were always the victims. My ancestors became the victims ever since they were forcefully removed from their homeland, mistreated and sold into slavery. They suffered at the hands of their oppressor, the British. Nonetheless, they were prepared to stay and fight until they were victorious and win a battle that meant their freedom.

The time has come for the war to end; the British called the truce. They wanted the war to end. Just as they started the attack, they called for it to be over.

The treaty is a "Blood Treaty", said Samuel.

"What do you mean by that daddy"?

Kojo did not trust the British soldiers and therefore Kojo asked for a "Blood Treaty". This was Samuel's explanation. Kojo was willing to cut his wrist to draw blood and wanted the "white man" to do the same. He said that they mixed the blood from their wounds and drank the mixture.

"How did they catch the blood to mix it"? I asked. "They caught the blood in a calabash", said Samuel. Kojo and the "white man" each then drank from the mixed blood. I thought this was bizarre. He also said that Kojo insisted that the "white man" drink first. He said that Kojo had to be sure that the "white man" was serious about the truce.

Samuel said that blood is important and meant that the Treaty was now good. Neither Kojo nor the British had a Seal or Stamp so it was smart that Kojo made such a request. The immediacy with which the British surrendered did not afford the time to produce a Seal. Kojo's aim however was to make the Treaty credible. Samuel said that Kojo did not trust them. Is it possible that the British misguided them already? He also said that Kojo and Nanny agreed to accept land settlement long before the war ended. After so many years away from Africa, a return to the Mother Land was not prudent it seems. They were visionaries and recognized the value of land ownership. There was no compensation befitting as a settlement for the horror endured; however, an identified place of abode and the right to freedom and self-government were considered acceptable.

Samuel said that when the British surrendered, they offered Kojo and Nanny all of Jamaica. He said, "The British were so happy to end the war that when the word came from England to end the war, the British was willing to give Kojo and his men all of Jamaica; anything to stop the defense of the African soldiers. Kojo requested all the lands in the Cockpit Country from seacoast to seacoast"

My ancestors were not greedy. Why take more than you need. Not all the Africans in Jamaica were engaged in the fight for freedom and they should have a place to live too. He said that Nanny did not live to see the Peace Treaty signed. He said that she fell ill on her way from

Portland to Accompong and died before she reached Accompong; she was buried in Accompong. I have heard many stories that contradict my father's; however, my writing only shares what my father said.

Peace cave was near to Kojo's house in Old Town. It was at Peace Cave that the Treaty of 1738 was signed. I have since climbed into Peace Cave to experience it. The cave, Peace Cave, can accommodate about twelve adults. You have to bend down when you are inside so I believe it's not best for people taller than six feet. My father said the Maroons would climb into the cave and await the British soldiers. Outside the cave there was a stone and each time a soldier stepped on the stone the stone clapped and Kojo and those inside would know how many soldiers passed. I believe that my ancestors selected this area because of the natural engineering features. There are many caves throughout the Cockpit Mountains. During the eighty years of fighting, my ancestors studied and recorded landmarks, water sources, trails and lookout points and housing.

Peace Cave

Those inside would know how many soldiers passed. There was also a small hole on the left side of the cave. This hole was close to the ground and was a portal that allowed a beam of light into the cave. A shadow was cast if any object crossed the portal. The clap of the stone together with the shadow that was cast, were excellent markers that the Africans used to determine how to counter attack. How clever of the African soldiers. These markers are still there to this day. I believe that these areas had to be disguised and kept clean at all times.

FAMILY

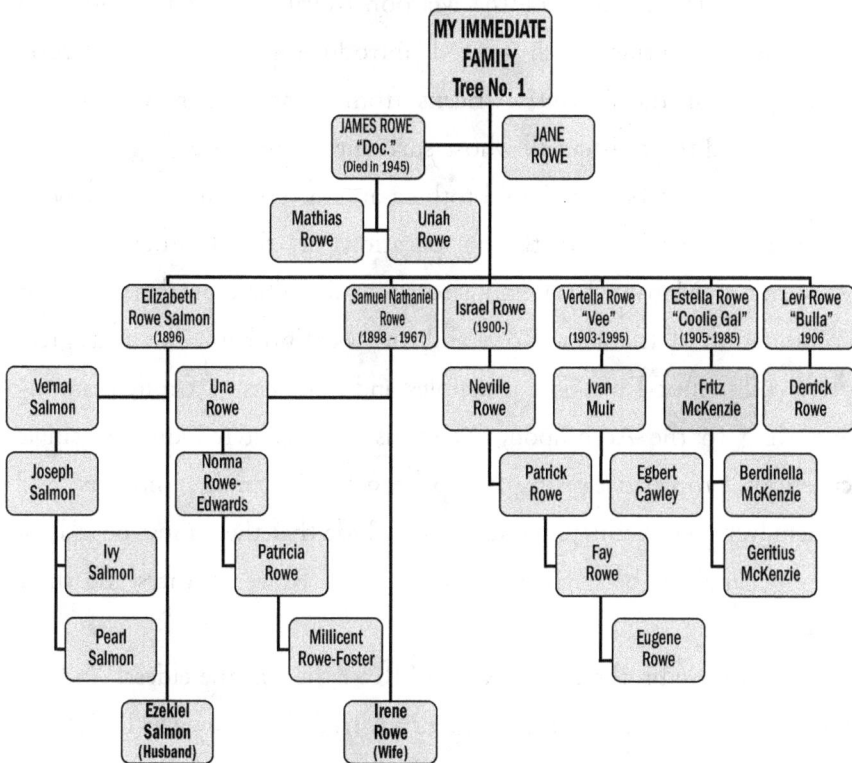

Samuel told us that the Accompong Maroons are one "Royal Family". He chuckled and smiled at the same time when he said this. We were old enough to understand what the term "Royal Family" meant. Theirs was an organized institution of marriage that promulgated the marriage between cousins, aunts and uncles. As far as I was concerned, Samuel need not elaborate on this information. After all, I knew that Queen Elizabeth was married to her cousin, the Duke of Edinburgh. This Royal couple represented the accepted state of intermarriage. Not only were these cousins married but also their marriage yielded children. If the practice of intermarriage is good for the British Royal Family then certainly it is good for my African ancestors; good in the sense that society will not ridicule such an institution; and that my African ancestors will not be labeled in any fashion or form.

So who is a member of the Maroon Royal Family? This question continues to surface each time I introduce myself as a Maroon descendant of the Ashanti Africans from Ghana. There were twelve brothers and three sisters all whose surnames were Rowe.

Samuel reports that these brothers and sisters were in one way or another responsible for the propagation of the Maroon race in Accompong Maroon Town and across Jamaica. These brothers were the continuation of the name Rowe and they were probably the great great grandchildren of Kojo. The principles and practices of family planning according to the Accompong Maroons were centered on one single criterion: propagate, propagate, propagate. Naturally, mothers and fathers were very young; therefore, I conclude that there must be at least three generations between the famous twelve Rowe brothers and three Rowe sisters.

The twelve brothers were Richard Rowe; he was the eldest. And the brothers were James, Peter, Jack, Henry Alfred also known as Pa Coolie,

Emmanuel-Baba, Esau also known as Ba Pigeon, Edgar, Jeffrey, Thomas, Charles and Masa Bundu. The three sisters were Matilda, Susan and Betsy. Samuel said Rowe is the slave name given to Kojo. Samuel told us that Kojo's slave name was Henry Octavos Rowe.

Samuel smiled again. "We are one royal family." The chuckle ended with a lingering smile. Two hundred and seventy years since the war was won against the British and the surname Rowe remains the most common name in Accompong. I have discovered lately that this Rowe name can be found in areas such as Thornton, Bagdal Mountain, Aberdeen, Whitehall, Siloah, Windsor, Cooks bottom, Garlands and South St. Elizabeth, Portland. I am not saying that other Maroon surnames are nonexistent. What I am saying is that it is the Rowe name however, that is indigenous in Accompong Town. This name is intertwined in every Maroon family in Accompong and outside Accompong.

The genealogy of other Accompong Maroon families will be discussed in my next writing. This name Rowe can be found in other areas in the Cockpit Country and all over Jamaica. Samuel said he wanted to be sure that we did not marry or have children with a cousin. He was not a supporter of the practice of intermarriage. This was his reason to tell us that anywhere we go in Jamaica and find someone with the surname Rowe; we should know that the person is a relative and descended from an Accompong Maroon. Samuel was sure of this like he was of everything else about our ancestors. If these men were born in Accompong how then was the name spread across the Island of Jamaica?

I learned the answer to this question a few years ago. Miss Leitha, an Accompong Maroon, told me that the brothers were skilled manufacturers of twisted ropes. The rope was made from the bark of the trumpet tree. The tree was cut down close to the root. After the tree fell, the men beat the trunk from the base to the top of the tree. This process made removal of the bark easy. The bark was then peeled and hung to dry; the dried bark was then plaited and twisted into a rope. This was the strongest rope on the market. The men planted a tree for every tree that was cut down. The Maroons were the first people and community in Jamaica to practice sustainable forestry. They planted a tree for every tree removed.

Where is the link between the manufacture of ropes and the spread of the Maroon lineage specifically the name Rowe? Soon after the Treaty was signed the Accompong Maroons, mostly these twelve brothers, exercised their freedom and traveled outside of Accompong Town to seek markets for the rope. They traveled all over Jamaica and they were away from home for long periods. What happened while they were away from home was therefore summed up in Samuels's statement, "anywhere you go in Jamaica and you find someone with the name Rowe you are related to the person." My immature mind accepted this statement. I had absolutely no reason to doubt the accuracy of his statement. I guess this fact was more appealing to me at that time in both its delivery and content. The feeling of belonging to a "big" family gave me a special sense of purpose. It was a plan to find and trace all these Maroon descendants.

My grandfather, James, was one of the twelve brothers and his travel to sell rope routed him to a District in St. Elizabeth called New Market at a place known as Nightingale Grove. Interestingly enough my mother Irene Rebecca Rowe nee Thomas was from Nightingale Grove. I wonder how my father met my mother. Were they practicing the same rope migration and marriage process of my ancestors? My grandfather James Rowe fathered a son Matthias Selvin Rowe. Uncle Selvin's mother was also from Nightingale Grove in New Market. She was a cousin of my mother. James took Uncle Selvin's mother to Accompong where Uncle Selvin was born. James Rowe's first wife, Jane Rowe my grandmother, died after the birth of another uncle, Uncle Levi, or Bulla as all affectionately called him. Aunt Betsy, who was the oldest of all the children of James and Jane Rowe, nurtured bulla and his other siblings. My cousin Fitz McKenzie, Aunt Coolie's son, is the one who told me this.

20

THE GOVERNMENT, LAW AND ORDER OF TRELAWNY TOWN MAROONS, ACCOMPONG STATE

After the Peace Treaty was signed, Kojo was the first leader of the Trelawny Town Maroons Accompong State. Daddy said that Accompong was a brother of Kojo and he was the second leader of the Maroons. The town Accompong is named after this brother of Kojo. The leaders were given the honorary title as Chief. I am not sure at what time that subsequent Leaders were called Colonel, a Colonial title, but that is what the leader is called today.

The Treaty gave the Maroons the right to govern themselves, select a leader, create their laws, secure their territory and carry arms. In 2009, the Jamaican Government acknowledged the rights of the Accompong Maroons when they refused to offer financial support and assist in the conduct of the Accompong Maroon election. The Accompong Maroons took charge and conducted their election. This was the first time since 1945 that the Trelawny Town Maroons managed and conducted their election. I will speak more about this election in my next writing as I share with the public our story.

Samuel said that the voting procedure was simple. The elders of the Town selected the persons best suited as colonel. Each candidate was asked to post money before the election. The people voted for the Chief with a show of hands. The candidate with the largest show of hands was declared the winner and leader and appointed as the Chief. It was indeed a simple procedure; one that sounds archaic in today's world of corruption and tribalism. Nevertheless, I believe the showing of hands clearly displayed the strong character, honesty, unity and transparency that prevailed among our ancestors. There was nothing to hide or fear when it was time to select their leader. They truly understood the meaning of democracy. Theirs was an efficient cost effective voting system that discouraged bribery of any kind. According to Samuel, our ancestors understood good governance. The leaders understood the meaning of integrity and honesty. They valued the individual Maroon character and wanted the spirit of truth and honesty to prevail. Those leaders led by example. The Chief, the Council of elders, past Chiefs, women and men of the community, united in an organizational system that encouraged an all-inclusive practice of management. They took the lead from Kojo and Nanny and followed their good example in leadership style.

Samuel said Kojo settled disputes in Accompong. The cat-o-nine was used as a form of punishment for serious crimes, while community service was prescribed for other petty offenses.

This list of Accompong Maroon Colonels that follows was shared with me by Mr. Harris Cawley, himself a past Colonel of the Trelawney Town Maroons Accompong State.

Kojo

Accompong. The Town Accompong is named after Accompong who is a brother of Kojo and Nanny. He ruled as chief after the death of Kojo.

Austin

White

T.Cross

H.D.Rowe

R.J.McLeod

K.T.Wright

H.E.Wright

H.R.Rowe was one of the twelve brothers, and my grand uncle. He was the famous Henry Octavius Rowe also known as Pa Coolie. Stories are told that Pa Coolie was the "best" Colonel in Accompong. My cousin told me that Pa Coolie was responsible for "cleaning up" Accompong Town and enforced law and order in the community. Prior to this clean up, ping wing macaw and rose apple trees were all over. Pigs roamed the land. Pa Coolie and his team cleaned the access areas and made roads throughout the community. His old house is at Riverhole. Uncle Egbert told me that Colonel Rowe was requested to report to Kings House by the then Governor Denham. Colonel Rowe along with a delegation of Maroons reported to Kings House. The meeting was heated and Colonel Rowe declared emphatically that the Government should leave Maroon lands alone. Uncle Egbert told me that when Colonel Rowe spoke and stomped his feet the place shook. Governor Denham ended the meeting. Sometime soon after the meeting, Governor Denham died, and was buried at sea. This happened sometime between 1937 and 1939. Norman Manley and his wife Edna Manley also visited Colonel Rowe at his home in Riverhole.

Walter I Robertson

Isaac Myles

Thomas J. Cawley. He was known as the most decorated Colonel.

C. Reid

Martin Luther Wright was the longest reigning Colonel. His term reportedly lasted for seventeen years.

Meredie Rowe

Sidney Peddie

Ferron Williams is the Colonel at the time this writing, September 2010.

CONCLUSION

The lack of documentation of a powerful story about the black people in the Caribbean has been used to derail our African identity. The historians are not telling the history and events of the war that the British lost. What we experienced during an era in history when Africans fought together for their freedom against all odds is only being reduced to the story of a heroine named Nanny.

Her astute abilities as a Commander-in-Chief are omitted and she is removed from her conjoint role in the battle with her brother Kojo and other Maroons. What is the reason for this omission and is it the reason why Samuel was constantly talking about Nanny and Kojo? Nanny is a heroine and Kojo is a hero. The labels of heroine and hero and the recognition of these Ashanti African ancestors are bigger than two mere status symbols for Jamaican people. Their recognition must result in the constant unfolding and positive reminder of our potential. As African people, we must understand that these ancestors passed through a difficult, horrid period. They deserve the recognition of their success during this ordeal. The knowledge of what our ancestors fought to overcome would stick to our Spirit for generations to come.

I sympathize with my fellow Maroons who through no fault of their own missed the familial richness of my experience. Those of you who have been so privileged as I have been, please tell what you know as told to you by your elders. A phrase says "Out of sight out of mind." I encourage you to keep the flame of our rich heritage glowing by telling what you know, not what others are writing about us. We must make a determination to shake off all the negative labels that we have allowed others to use to shape our destiny. Instead, think of the mastery of our ancestors and dare to believe in the God of our ancestors and believe in ourselves. Dare to believe that we have yet to visualize the potential of us as a people and be determined to chart a path to success. Our ancestors started the race; we only have to continue with determination.

We lack a sense of history and the pride that emanates from our ancestral accomplishments. Marcus Mosiah Garvey said "Our ancestors were winners. Live as our ancestors did. When you contemplate a loss, you immediately shut your door to the endless possibilities for success, opportunities and victory that is waiting for you behind the door."

What is to be expected if we were to fight one day for justice or spend some time in the shoe of our ancestors. We live in a world of endless opportunities and possibilities. This world of endless possibilities escapes our self-enforced myopic view of our incapabilities. We are prisoners to our environment and allow the system that surrounds us to arrest our potential and therefore shape our destiny. We allow others to build our self-esteem with material things and confuse our identity with false labels. Not all of us will be a Kojo or a Nanny, but with a sincere heart, we can learn how to follow in the footsteps of our positive leaders.

Somewhere between 1738 and now, an insidious onset of fear has crept into the minds of some Maroon descendants and we languish as we wait for the "Knight in Shining Armour" to come to our rescue. There is no such a person. We owe it our children and the generations to come to put us on track again.

"The heart of man is desperately wicked," says the Good Book. Man's greed and indifference designed and perpetuated atrocities such as the Atlantic Slave Trade. There is abundance in the world and we can live life abundantly only if we as a people embrace the Truth. The truth is that God is Love. We must remove all the shackles of fear, hate, envy, greed, strife, covetousness and ignorance. Our ancestors discarded these shackles in order to stay true to the course of success.

From the 18th Century, 1738 precisely, to the present 21st Century the year 2010 and into the beyond our spirit will live. The spirit of our African ancestors lives. In this period of seeming chaos lie many great opportunities and endless possibilities for true believers. We must embrace the truth like our African ancestors. Do not only think "outside of the box" but also with careful detailed conscious planning, break loose and remove the "box".

We must dare ourselves to pattern the life of the beautiful butterfly and break forth from the cocoon. Our ancestors knew how to break the cocoon. It is because of their determination and smarts that our ancestors have produced educators, researchers, lawyers, nurses, doctors, craftsmen and women builders, cooks, preachers and many more. Above all, we are created in God's image. Let us embrace that truth and collectively purpose in our hearts to discard anything that separates us from the love and blessings and grace of God. Trelawny Town Maroons are sovereign and we have the right to govern ourselves as stated by the Treaty of 1738-39. Foolish acts by the Maroons have contributed to the questioning of our sovereignty.

The call to you my Maroon brothers and sisters throughout the Diaspora is to "emancipate your mind from mental slavery" as Bob Marley so implored as he sung the words of Marcus Mosiah Garvey. The battle for our continued success starts in our minds. Our ancestors knew that and refused to fall prey to the subtle cheap prescription of "I can'tism". When he was faced with the demonic spirit of racism and racial injustice, Marcus Mosiah Garvey embraced the spirit of truth and stayed the course of his mission. Martin Luther King received visions and prophesied about that Spirit, the spirit of hope; Nelson Mandela refused to bow to an insane system called apartheid and demonstrated the potential of the Spirit. Today, Barak Obama represents the embodiment of all. Obama in this time is commanded and compelled to serve. He understands the call to yield in obedience to the Spirit as he latches on to the grace of God. We can believe in grace. It is a hope we must all walk in.

We have a responsibility to make the choice to pass on to our children the legacy given to us by our ancestors. The legacy removes and demolishes the negative stereotype of Maroon Africans and other people of African descent. Samuel did just that. Imagine if every parent or responsible adult purposed to walk in the potential of the Spirit of God. Imagine if we dare to believe that we could do all things through Christ who strengthens us. Imagine if we believe that God will supply all of our needs according to his riches in glory through Christ Jesus. Imagine all the people living life in peace, says John Lennon. The good thing is that we need not imagine but purpose to take hold of our present day situation and be responsible for our beliefs and actions. Having done all to stand.

What are we leaving for our children? Samuel shared many of life's lessons with us. One of his favourite lessons was, "Jack Panya never cry for feather he cry for long life." Jackpanya is a bird that is similar to a fowl. The body of the bird is feathered during the winter season and loses its feather during the summer months. Daddy constantly reminded us not to focus on the problem. Instead he encouraged us to believe in the gift of life, the present. That is why it is called the PRESENT. Only the living spirit can enjoy the gift of today, the gift of now. Like Jack Panya, as long as there is life then we can hope for a favourable outcome. Like our ancestors, we must first understand the enemy lies within us. Know what external forces want to do to us. Keep in our focus at all times our position as achievers. Stay steadfast to our goal of achieving and remember we must maintain our character as we succeed. I write to the keepers of our children and charge all to work diligently to mold the dreams of our children's future. I ask parents, family members, teachers and responsible adults to purposely tell our Maroon African story and encourage our young ones to embrace their identity as African Maroons: A people with dignity, a proud past and a blessed future.

I apologize to my children for my benign omission and neglect to expose them to the power of living in the true Spiritual connection. Samuel did this by telling us the story of our ancestors. He did that by example as he constantly read his bible. How do we preserve without destroying? The challenge is to avoid exploitation as we grapple for economic sustainability. We are not enslaved however; we have become slaves to a domesticated environment. How do we preserve? We preserve by refusing to be beggars. How do we preserve? We preserve by educating our children and ourselves. How do we preserve? We preserve by staying honest and working hard.

Samuel had us to say this prayer every night before going to bed.

Gentle Jesus meek and mild
Look upon a little child
Pity my simplicity
Suffer me to come to thee.
Feign I would to thee be brought
If I should die before I wake
I pray the Lord my soul to take.

When I was a child, I had difficulty saying the words, "If I should die before I wake." I was afraid to pray this prayer because the words seemed to link me to this abysmal place called death. I had no idea what happened after death. Samuel, however, had his plans for his burial. He was always telling us to wrap his body and bury it in an open grave. Maybe this was some custom. I did not explore this matter. I believe that to him the body after death was immaterial to the struggle, therefore, he was teaching us to place our emphasis on life. Let the life we live truly represent who we are as great Africans from the Motherland Africa.

My prayers now center on the Spirit of the Living God as I contemplate the depth and spirit of my African Ashanti ancestors.

It is my hope that this generation of Maroons in Jamaica will begin to recognize their powerful positive identity, the importance of unity and the benefits that come when we know who we are and embrace our history, heritage and culture. I speak especially to Accompong Maroons and those from Accompong living outside the Accompong community. We must understand that we have a rich legacy and because of this, many envy us. I call on my fellow Maroons and this new generation of Maroons to grasp with passion the importance of our heritage and be determined to live our history, hold on to our legacy and pass them on to the next generation. Our tangible legacy, our land, is for the "born and the unborn".

Rock near Peace Cave

A close-up of foliage in area called Ambush

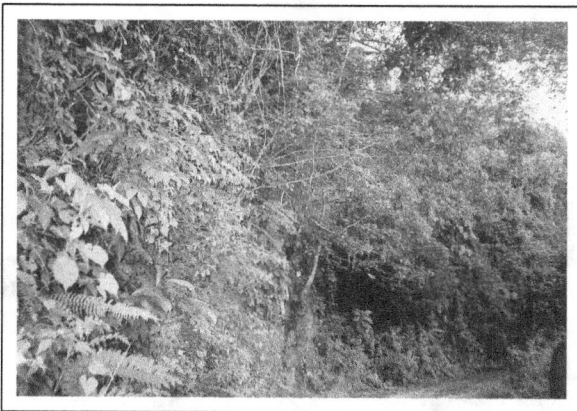

Foliage in area called Ambush

View of foliage from Old Town

View from Old Town

Small area of the Cockpit - View
from Kindah

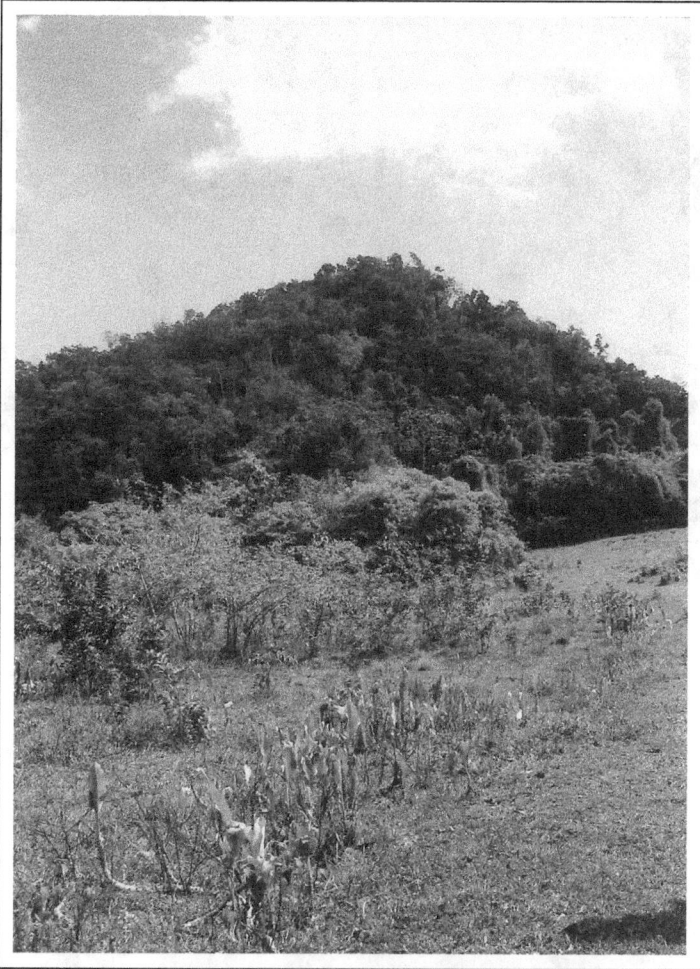

A Close-Up of Foliage Near Peace Cave

On the road to Kindah

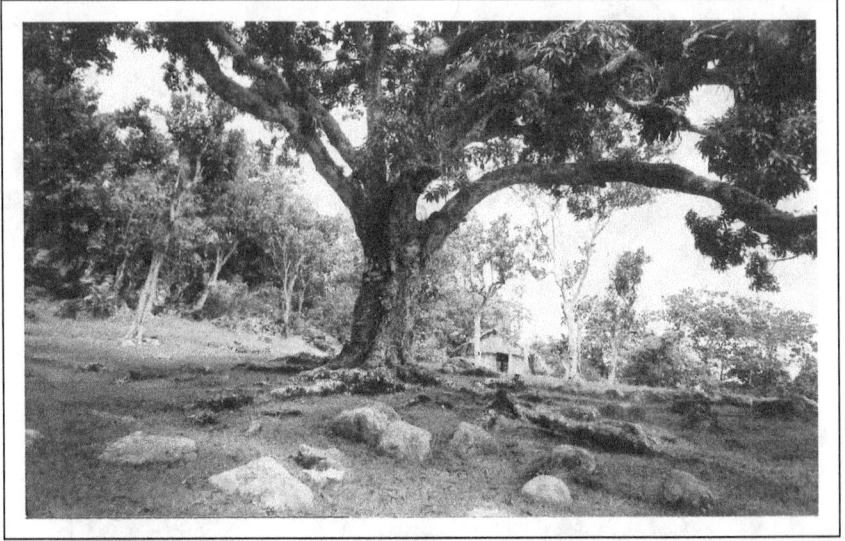

Kindah

BIBLIOGRAPHY

Augier, F.R., S.C.Gordon, D.G. Hall, M. Reckford, *The Making of the West Indies*, Longman Publishing 1960

Bilby, Kenneth M., *True Born Maroons*. Ian Randle Publishers, Kingston. Miami 2006

Brathwaite, Kamau, *The Development of Creole Society in Jamaica 1770-1820*. Ian Randle Publishers. Kingston. Miami 2005

Black, Clinton V. *HISTORY OF JAMAICA*, LONDON AND GLASGOW COLLINS CLEAR-TYPE PRESS, 1958

Campbell, Mavis, *The Maroons of Jamaica 1655-1796: A History of Resistance Collaboration & Betrayal.* African World Press 1990

Carey, Beverly, *The Maroon Story: The Authentic and Original History of the Maroons in the History of Jamaica 1490-1880*

Falconbridge, Alexander, *An Account of the Slave Trade on the Coast of Africa*. London 1788

Harris, Joseph E., *AFRICANS AND THEIR HISTORY*, A Mentor Book, August 1972

Knight, Franklin W., The Caribbean *The Genesis of A Fragmented Nationalism*, New York. Oxford University Press. 1978

Beckles, Hilary McD and Verene A. Shepherd, *TRADING SOULS EUROPE'S TRANSATLTNTIC TRADE IN AFRICANS,*

ABICENTENNIAL CARIBBEAN REFLECTION, Ian Randle
Publishers Kingston. Miami 2007

Patterson, Orlando, <u>The Sociology of Slavery: An Analysis of</u>
<u>the Origin, Development and Structure of Negro Slave Society</u>
<u>in Jamaica.</u> London: Maggibbon & Kee 1967I

Shepherd, Verene A, *I Want to disturb My Neighbour, Lectures*
on Slavery, Emancipation and Postcolonial Jamaica, Ian
Randle Publishers, Kingston. Miami 2007

Williams, Eric, *'FROM COLUMBUS TO CASTRO: THE HISTORY*
OF THE CARIBBEAN 1492-1969, Andre' Deutsch 1970